Quest for the Whooperdink

A Play with Music

A.H. Teacey

Samuel French - London
New York - Sydney - Toronto - Hollywood

Copyright © 1984 by Samuel French Ltd
All Rights Reserved

QUEST FOR THE WHOOPERDINK is fully protected under the copyright laws of the British Commonwealth, including Canada, the United States of America, and all other countries of the Copyright Union. All rights, including professional and amateur stage productions, recitation, lecturing, public reading, motion picture, radio broadcasting, television and the rights of translation into foreign languages are strictly reserved.

ISBN 978-0-573-05070-1

www.samuelfrench.co.uk
www.samuelfrench.com

For Amateur Production Enquiries

United Kingdom and World excluding North America

plays@samuelfrench.co.uk

020 7255 4302/01

Each title is subject to availability from Samuel French, depending upon country of performance.

CAUTION: Professional and amateur producers are hereby warned that QUEST FOR THE WHOOPERDINK is subject to a licensing fee. Publication of this play does not imply availability for performance. Both amateurs and professionals considering a production are strongly advised to apply to the appropriate agent before starting rehearsals, advertising, or booking a theatre. A licensing fee must be paid whether the title is presented for charity or gain and whether or not admission is charged.

No one shall make any changes in this title for the purpose of production. No part of this book may be reproduced, stored in a retrieval system, or transmitted in any form, by any means, now known or yet to be invented, including mechanical, electronic, photocopying, recording, videotaping, or otherwise, without the prior written permission of the publisher. No one shall upload this title, or part of this title, to any social media websites.

The right of A.H. Teacey to be identified as author of this work has been asserted in accordance with Section 77 of the Copyright, Designs and Patents Act 1988.

CHARACTERS

Professor Potterton, a scientist
Crystal, his daughter
Salmonella, the wicked witch
Seth, her son
The Urgles
The Guardian of the Fiery Cave
The Snowflake Maker
The Whooperdink

ACT I	SCENE 1	Professor Potterton's Laboratory
	SCENE 2	Salmonella's Parlour
	SCENE 3	The Urgle Camp
	SCENE 4	Outside the Fiery Cave
	SCENE 5	Beyond the Fiery Cave
	SCENE 6	The Snowy Plains
ACT II	SCENE 1	The Urgle Camp
	SCENE 2	The Snowy Plains
	SCENE 3	The Urgle Camp
	SCENE 4	Outside the Fiery Cave
	SCENE 5	The Snowy Plains

AUTHOR'S NOTE

In general the text is self-explanatory; however the following notes may be of use.

CHARACTERS

The **Professor**'s two chief attributes are a keen (perhaps over-) enthusiasm and an ability to become totally absorbed in whatever has taken his attention. This occasionally frustrates his daughter **Crystal**, who as the heroine is attractive both physically and by nature. It is she who ultimately brings about the saving of **Seth**, who though often a figure of ridicule and fun is in the true sense of the word pathetic, and ought to have the sympathy of the audience throughout.

His mother, **Salmonella** is larger-than-life and truly villainous, but her character is partly explained and driven by the frustration of having to cope with Seth for twenty years. She, too, must be capable of undergoing an improving transformation acceptable to the audience. The **Snowflake Maker** is seen here as an elderly cockney whose melancholic exterior hides a heart of gold. He, like Seth, is in need of Crystal's warmth to bring out his best. The **Guardian** ought to be a figure of awe, rather than of fear. His physique, costume and voice ought to combine to create a spectacular and awe-inspiring effect. He ought to have the detached superiority of a god, and imply a commensurate power.

The **Urgles** are whatever the costume designer makes of them. They need to be other-worldly, to contrast with the humans in the script, yet with foibles and characteristics recognizeable to all. Finally the **Whooperdink** is as described in the text, and another opportunity for the costume designer. The bird ought to be vulnerable and instantly lovable.

STAGING

Though conceived for theatre-in-the-round, the play can be *staged* perfectly well in other ways, with as much or as little set as is required. The bare essentials are indicated in the text, but these can be supplemented. Lighting can be used to suggest different locations, and in this respect a snowflake effect light is commercially available which adds atmosphere to the snowy plains. *Lighting* can also supplement such sequences as the telling of the curse and the casting of the magic snowflakes. *Effects* too can be as simple or as complex as required or resources permit. The explosive devices and flares necessary for the laboratory and cave are widely available commercially; and flourescent paint and/or ultra-violet lighting can be used to create a "glowing" tail feather. The magic snow can be released either by the Snowflake Maker or from above, depending on the facilities available. *Costumes* are very much a matter of choice.

MUSIC

The music for the songs "The Whooperdink", "Snowflake", and "The Jelly Baby Song" will be found on pages 54, 56, and 59. **Please note that a licence issued by Samuel French Ltd to perform this play only includes permission to use these songs.**

The notice printed below on behalf of the Performing Right Society should be carefully read if any other copyright music is to be used in this play.

The following statement concerning the use of music is printed here on behalf of the Performing Right Society Ltd, by whom it was supplied

The permission of the owner of the performing right in copyright music must be obtained before any public performance may be given, whether in conjunction with a play or sketch or otherwise, and this permission is just as necessary for amateur performances as for professional. The majority of copyright musical works (other than oratorios, musical plays and similar dramatico-musical works) are controlled in the British Commonwealth by the PERFORMING RIGHT SOCIETY LTD, 29-33 BERNERS STREET, LONDON W1P 4AA.

The Society's practice is to issue licences authorizing the use of its repertoire to the proprietors of premises at which music is publicly performed, or, alternatively, to the organizers of musical entertainments, but the Society does not require payment of fees by performers as such. Producers or promoters of plays, sketches, etc., at which music is to be performed, during or after the play or sketch, should ascertain whether the premises at which their performances are to be given are covered by a licence issued by the Society, and if they are not, should make application to the Society for particulars as to the fee payable.

ACT I*

Scene 1

Professor Potterton's Laboratory

There is a laboratory bench R, *with various glassware, specimen jars, a glass flask, a bottle of "nitrate", a bottle of "potash", a bottle of "sulphuric acid", and a cloth.* L *is a bookshelf containing books*

The Lights come up on Professor Potterton working on an experiment at his bench and humming merrily to himself. He takes a step back towards C *and bends away with his hands over his ears. There is a flash and bang from the bench as the experiment explodes*

Professor Botheration! It always hapens, every time I add the nitrate solution to the potash it does that. Well, that's wrecked my recticule. (*He picks up the cloth from the bench and begins to mop up the mess on the floor. He spots something moving across the floor and begins to pursue it on his hands and knees. During this sequence his grunts of disgust change to those of interest in the creepy-crawly*) Ugh! Urgh ... Umm ... Ohhhh ... Ahhh ...

Crystal, his daughter, enters L *with a letter*

Crystal Father?
Professor Just a minute ...
Crystal What are you looking at?
Professor I'm not looking at anything at the moment, I can't see it. I'm trying to catch an earwiggle-wriggle—or is it an earwriggle-wiggle? Anyway, whatever you are, I want you. Come along, my beauty!
Crystal Mail, Father.
Professor I'm not bothered whether it's male or female, I haven't got either in my collection.
Crystal (*moving to the bench*) It's a letter for you, Father.
Professor Ah! There we are. (*He captures creepy crawly, and moves to the bench to place the specimen in a specimen jar*) You read it to me.
Crystal (*reading the letter*) "Dear Percival, As I was working on my thesis on 'Creatures, Crustacea and Other Creepy-Crawlies', I caught sight of a lesser black-backed, spotted-tail, snitch-nose louse and immediately I thought of you. I decided to write and let you know of my latest discovery in order to see if you had time to track it down. Whilst travelling through Urgleland on my autumn expedition I came across some rather unusual footprints. I then found a broken toenail which led me to wonder whether I was at last on the track of something most unusual. When I then found

---

*N.B. Paragraph 3 on page ii of this Acting Edition regarding photocopying and video-recording should be carefully read.

devastated strawberry plants I felt sure I was at last on the track of the Metaphoria Zygosa, a member of the Zychosorium species—in other words, a Whooperdink!"

At the mention of the word "Whooperdink" the Professor stops what he is doing, snatches the letter and dances up and down with it with excitement

Professor Whooperdink! Whooperdink! Ohh, this is fantastic, absolutely fantastic, absolutely incredible!
Crystal What's a Whooperdink?
Professor A Whooperdink? It's a creature about—oh—so high, slightly wider at the bottom than the top, and it has an enormously long nose which it uses for sucking up jam, which is its speciality. It goes down and ducks into it (*he mimes the actions*)—mmmm—and then sucks at the jam! It's absolutely splendid! It's not been seen for hundreds of years, and now, at last... oh, it's incredible... absolutely fantastic!
Crystal What else does the letter say?
Professor (*returning to the letter*) "... Whooperdink! Yes, really, a Whooperdink. I wanted to follow the tracks further, but caught a touch of the bungo-bungos"—poor lad, poor lad—"so I am laid up in bed." Send him a card, Crystal, will you? "So, potter on, Potterton! Don't delay, drop everything and get on the trail! Yours, Reginald Wouldbegood. PS. I discovered that, though very timid, the Urgles of Urgleland can be won over by tempting them with sweet things. They seem particularly fond of jelly babies, so I advise you to take along a good supply. PPS. Map overleaf. PPPS. Toenail enclosed." Toenail? Toenail.
Crystal Toenail...

They search for the toenail on the floor

Professor Where were you when you opened the letter?
Crystal By the bench.

They go over to the bench and find the toenail in the bottom of one of the Professor's flasks. The letter is left on the bench

Father, the bottom of this flask—there's a thing in the bottom of it. (*She holds it up*)

Professor Good Lord, it's a broken toenail.
Crystal Can you get it out?
Professor Er—no.
Crystal Oh.
Professor I think Reggie's tracking of the Whooperdink must be one of the most important discoveries of the past two hundred years. (*He moves to pick up a reference book from the shelf* L) Just think—a Whooperdink! (*He looks at the book*) Whooperdink—page three-nine-two—yes, here we are. "A rare bird, thought to be extinct, it stands some one hundred and twenty centimetres tall, and has the unusual feature of being a three-toed palmipede with a prehensile proboscis. Its colouration is blue-purple, except for a crest and tail of bright yellow feathers. A timid creature, it has rarely

Act I, Scene 1   3

been seen; registered sightings have been made in three places only—Bonzola, Urgleland and Flixton-by-the-Sea. The bird can be easily identified by its call, a strange whooping sound, which gives the creature its name." Oh, isn't it exciting. I can hardly wait! Let's pack immediately. Drop everything, he said—so drop it!

Crystal is still holding the flask

No! don't drop that!
Crystal (*putting the flask down on the bench*) It's all right, Father, I wasn't going to drop it.
Professor Come on then, let's get packed!
Crystal Where is Urgleland?
Professor Well, it's—well, it's ... well, let's have a look at the map. (*He goes to the bench*)

They look at the map together

Crystal It looks as though we will have to go through the Fiery Cave then across the Snowy Plains to get there; I'll start packing our things.
Professor Yes do, there's a good girl; I'll start to get my equipment together.

The Professor exits R and Crystal exits L and each returns with a bag which they place C. Then, from various points around and off stage, they gather their items, counting them off as they do so

Professor Magnifying glass ...
Crystal Mosquito net ...
Professor Compass ...
Crystal Cardigans ...
Professor Specimen jars ...
Crystal Sunhats ...
Professor Retort ...
Crystal Rug ...
Professor Tripod ...
Crystal Thermos flask ...
Professor Sextant ...
Crystal Sunglasses ...
Professor Geological hammer ....
Crystal Galoshes. ...
Professor Now, do we need the nitrate and potash? ...
Crystal No, Father.
Professor I'd better take them—oh, and the sulphuric acid.
Crystal Why, Father?
Professor In case we run into trouble. Mind you, of course if I tried to make it do that (*he looks at the bench*) it probably wouldn't. (*He packs the chemicals into the bag, and has a final look round*) Ready?
Crystal Ready, Father.
Professor Have I got the letter and map?
Crystal (*picking it up from the bench*) Here it is, Father.
Professor Good girl. (*Folding the map and putting it into his pocket*) Good

heavens! The jelly babies! We must stop off at the local corner shop and buy a big bag of jelly babies. (*He picks up the bag*) Let's go! The Whooperdink is not extinct!

They exit

The Lights fade to Black-out

Scene 2

Salmonella's Parlour

Salmonella's magic bag, containing a reference book, a spell book and a wand, is R

The Lights come up on Seth, Salmonella's twenty-one year old son, sitting on the floor DL *facing the audience, eating dolly mixtures*

Salmonella dashes in R *carrying a magic telescope and wearing a witch's pointed hat and cape. The hat should have a collapsible top, converting it into a country hat, and the cape should be reversible, with a tweed pattern on the other side. This is to allow for the costume change required in Act I, Scene 5*

Salmonella Son, son!
Seth What?
Salmonella It's happened, the time has come; now the curse can be undone!
Seth What?
Salmonella The curse can be undone!
Seth What's a curse?
Salmonella A curse is a nasty spell.
Seth Spell? I can't spell anything. I can't even read.
Salmonella Not that sort of spell. (*She thumps him*) A magic spell, a witch's weapon. Like I used to give you those sweets.
Seth Ohh.
Salmonella And there's a spell, a curse, on you. Ever since you were born you've been stupid, and that's because—because a rival witch made it so. But today, I think the spell can be broken. Yes. Today's your birthday, you're twenty-one; and I think the curse can be undone.
Seth Mam, how many's twenty-one?
Salmonella How many's twenty-one? Don't you know? How many fingers have you got? Go on, count them.
Seth One ... two ...
Salmonella Three.
Seth Three ...
Salmonella Four.
Seth Four ...

And so on up to ten

Seth (*counting the finger he was pointing with*) Eleven——

Act I, Scene 2

Salmonella (*grabbing the finger, folding it into a fist and hitting Seth with it*) That's ten! Now we need some more. (*She starts to take his shoes and socks off; aside to the audience*) I'm not going to enjoy this. (*She begins on the toes*) Right.
Seth One...
Salmonella No, eleven!
Seth No, that's one, Mam!
Salmonella It's eleven.
Seth No—there's not eleven there, it's just one, Mam.
Salmonella (*slapping him*) ELEVEN!
Seth Eleven.
Salmonella Twelve...
Seth Twelve—ooh, that tickles. (*He giggles and writhes*)

Salmonella counts up to fifteen, with Seth laughing and counting at the same time

(*Holding up his little finger*) Mam, what was this one again?
Salmonella (*taking each hand, then one foot, in turn*) That was five, THAT was five, and THAT was five! Right, that's fifteen. Sixteen——
Seth This little piggy went to market, this little piggy——
Salmonella (*slapping him*) SIXTEEN!
Seth Sixteen.
Salmonella Seventeen.
Seth Seventeen.
Salmonella Eighteen.
Seth Eighteen. Hehehehehe.
Salmonella Nineteen. And that one makes twenty.

Pause. They look at one another

Borrow one of mine.

Seth Thank you.
Salmonella That's twenty-one. That's how many twenty-one is, right? That's how old you are. Put your shoes and socks back on.

He struggles to do so during the following

So—twenty-one years have passed, since that wicked curse was cast. You're twenty-one today.
Seth (*standing*) Today? Am I twenty-one today?
Salmonella Yes, it's your birthday. And the time has come to lift the curse. To begin with, we must——
Seth Mam...
Salmonella What?
Seth You know you said we had to lift the curse?
Salmonella Yes.
Seth Is it heavy?
Salmonella You are *so* stupid. I don't mean *lift* the curse, I mean take the curse away from you. Don't you want the curse lifted?

Seth shrugs, bewildered

I want the curse lifted! (*During this speech she circles round and round Seth, getting more and more angry*) For twenty-one years I've had to put up with you, look after you. You. Look at you. You loathsome creature; all these years, and what use have you been to me? I could have been a great witch, I could have travelled the world, using my powers and evil intent to cause death and destruction wherever I went. But instead I've had to stay here and look after you. Other witches have familiars—cats, frogs, toads, lizards, to help them with their spells, but all I have is stupid, stupid, sickening, soft and stupid you!

Seth Mam—can I have a birthday party?
Salmonella (*ignoring him*) When we've lifted the curse, we'll——
Seth Can I have a cake?
Seth When we've lifted the curse——
Seth Can I have a ball?
Salmonella When we've lifted the cu——
Seth Can I——
Salmonella SHUT UP AND LISTEN!

Pause. Seth sits

It's time I told you about the curse, and what it means. And how we're going to li—— er, remove it.

Seth settles to listen

Some months before you were born, I was out in the forest, gathering cobwebs and owl-droppings for the spell I was making.

The Lights fade to a green spot on Salmonella and eerie forest sounds are heard

Suddenly it grew very dark and cold; the leaves on the trees began to rustle and whisper, and a great wind blew up. Then, just as suddenly all was still.

The eerie sounds stop

Then a voice, a voice I knew very well, called to me from the skies.

Salmonella and Seth freeze in position; the voice comes out of the air

Voice   "Remember me, O Salmonella,
I'm your younger sister, Isabella.
I had to live for twenty years
With you, who caused me many tears.
Your cruel ways, your mystery,
Made my childhood a misery.
I had no witching powers then,
Although I often wished for them;
But wheels do turn, now I'm a witch too,
And I think more powerful now than you!
In my girlhood you made me suffer:
So now I'll make your son a duffer!
This curse shall last for twenty years;

Act I, Scene 2

> It shall begin and end in tears.
> At twenty-one then scan the skies—
> You may then have a great surprise.
> For what is gone is here again;
> Its magic may give him a brain.
> A whoop, a cry, a brush so light—
> Together these will make him bright."

The Lights return to normal and Salmonella and Seth unfreeze

Salmonella I hurried home and wrote it down, word for word, here in my spell book. Look. (*She gets her spell book and hands it to Seth*)

Seth stands up and takes the book, but looks at it upside down

Seth Are there any coloured pictures, Mam?

Salmonella (*grabbing back the book*) You fool. Why are you so stupid? Why can't you understand?

Seth One question at a time, Mam, please! (*He sits*)

Salmonella (*pacing to and fro*) The curse said: "At twenty-one then scan the skies". Today is your twenty-first birthday, and since dawn I've been searching through my magic telescope, and just now, not ten minutes ago, I saw it, the answer to the curse! "For what is gone is here again, its magic may give him a brain." The Whooperdink—one of the great magical beasts, it was thought to be extinct, but now that Professor has had a letter ... (*She takes a reference book from her bag*) Let's see ... Whooperdink ... page four-one-six ... (*She opens the book at this page only to find it has been torn out. In a rage she turns on Seth*) YOU! When did you tear it out? Where is it? What have you done with it?

Seth Mam, one question at a time!

Salmonella Time! Time! I'll give you time! Stand up!

Seth does so, and Salmonella fixes him in an awkward position

Right.
> My magic powers on you I stamp:
> Now stay like that and suffer cramp!

(*She points at him and there is a flash*)

Seth stays motionless in this position

Now, where was I? Oh yes, the Whooperdink. I must get to the Whooperdink, and use its magic to rid me of that curse. (*She looks forlornly at the book*) But *where* is its magic? What makes it magic? Bah, never mind that now—first I must *find* the Whooperdink. How can I do that? (*At this point she can involve the audience, if desired*) I know! I'll follow that Professor and his daughter! They will lead me to the Whooperdink! Come, son, we have to pack.

Seth doesn't move

We must collect our paraphenalia. (*She goes to Seth and shakes him*) Seth.

(*She then remembers her spell*) Oh.
> My former spell I now unmake
> But still I want your limbs to ache!

(*She points at him again and there is a flash*)

Seth comes to

Come on, we're going on a journey.
Seth Can we take a packed lunch?
Salmonella We'll need more than a packed lunch. We'll need lots of food. I'll order some now. (*She looks in her spell book*) Provisions ... provisions ... Ah, here it is: "Provisions: Spell For The Providing Of. First place your food bag in the kitchen." Seth, get the haversack.

Seth exits R *and returns with the haversack*

Take it to the kitchen, then come back here.

He takes the haversack off UL *and then enters*

Right. Now: (*reading from the book*)
> "For journeys far you need to take
> Lots of pies and meat and cake."

Seth (*going to her*) And sweets.
Salmonella (*reading*) "Fish and fowl and wine and mead
> These and plenty more you'll need."

Seth Especially sweets.
Salmonella (*reading*) "Let magic make all these decisions (*she casts a spell*)
> Now in your bag find your provisions."

Go and get the food bag, Seth.

Seth exits UL *and returns with the haversack, which is now full to bursting point*

Salmonella (*packing the reference book and spell book into her magic bag*) Come, son.
Seth (*searching through one of the haversack's outer pockets*) Mam!
Salmonella What now?
Seth I can't find any sweets!
Salmonella (*dipping into her bag for her wand; to herself or the audience*)
> My stupid son, 'tis all he eats
> For quietness sake—now there's your sweets.

(*Casting a spell, she aims it at the haversack*)

Salmonella exits UR

Seth rummages in an outer pocket and produces a tube of Smarties

Seth Oohh, thanks, Mam! (*Seeing she is not there*) Mam? Mam?

Seth, rather frightened, runs off after Salmonella UR

Fade to Black-out

Scene 3

The Urgle Camp

(*What follows is a synopsis of events that ought to take place. I have deliberately left it to each director to develop and elaborate the scene as he or she sees fit. Dialogue, if any, should consist entirely of the word "Urgle"; it is the actors' task to enable meaningful conversation to develop out of this single word. The ONLY other word used by Urgles is "Whooperdink".*)

The Lights come up to give a general blue effect on a deserted landscape

Gradually Urgles—timid but quick-moving creatures—creep out into the landscape. They begin to talk amongst themselves. A warning cry from one Urgle causes all the others to scatter. Eventually the Urgles, rather nervously, return, carrying a jam pan, a large wooden spoon, enormous strawberries and a chalice

The Chief Urgle summons the Urgles to the ritual of the Making of the Strawberry Jam. In full ceremonial the Urgles make the jam and it is clearly intended as some kind of offering to the Whooperdink

When the jam has been prepared, the Chief Urgle takes the chalice of jam off

All other Urgles wait with bated breath for the Chief to return. Slurping noises are heard off stage

The Chief Urgle returns with the empty chalice and indicates that the offering has once again been accepted

Joyous celebrations follow, and a dance to appropriate music surrounds the dismantling and removal of the jam-making equipment, which is then borne off by the happy crowd

Fade to Black-out

Scene 4

Outside the Fiery Cave

The Fiery Cave is a passage between two strange lands. The cave's entrance is UL *and its exit is* UR. *There is a large rock* UR *close by the exit*

The Lights come up on Crystal who enters wearily DL, *carrying her bag. She stops and looks around*

Crystal (*calling over her shoulder*) Come on, Father!
Professor (*off*) Just a minute, dear, I'm just looking at——
Professor } (*together*) { (*off, excitedly*) —another rock!
Crystal   { (*wearily*)
Crystal Father, we'll never get there at this rate.

The Professor enters DL, *carrying a bag and a rock*

Professor (*as he enters*) Absolutely splendid! I've never seen rocks like these before. Open the bag, dear; I'll just put a label on it and pop it in with the others.

Crystal Can't we stop and have something to eat now? Where are we anyway?

She looks at the map whilst the Professor continues to examine rocks

(*Looking at the cave entrance* UL) Oh, this must be——

The Guardian of the Fiery Cave suddenly appears at the entrance UL. *He carries two fire stones*

Crystal stands and stares at the Guardian. The Professor, oblivious, continues to search for more specimens DR.

Professor What have we here? This seems to be——
Crystal Father. Father!

The Professor turns and sees the Guardian. He too is awe-struck

Guardian I am the Guardian of the Fiery Cave. I have been here since time began, and my sole purpose is to guard the passage through the Fiery Cave. None may pass this way, save those who satisfy the Test of the Flames.
Professor Oh, I say, is this your cave? Those stalagmites look absolutely splendid, fascinating. Could I just——?

The Professor goes to enter the cave UL *but the Guardian bars his way*

Guardian None may pass this way, save those who satisfy the Test of the Flames.
Crystal Father!

The Professor and Crystal settle down to listen

Guardian The test is this: you must each take a fire stone and cast it into the cave. The stone will reveal whether you are good or evil. Only the good may pass. If the stone flares red, this shows you to be good, and you may proceed. If the stone flares green, then you are evil, and will be cast into the cave to feed the fiery flames. Do you wish to take the test?
Crystal We are good people, aren't we, Father?
Professor I think so, basically ... though once ...
Crystal (*anxiously*) What?
Professor Well ... once I took Henry Davidson's Aesculus Hippocastanum fruit.
Crystal What's that?
Professor What?
Crystal An Aescle ... Hippo ...?
Professor Aesculus Hippocastanum? A Horse Chestnut, of course.
Crystal A Horse Chestnut fruit—you mean a conker?
Professor Yes, that's right.
Crystal When was that?
Professor Oh, when I was—eight.
Crystal I don't think that counts.
Guardian Do you wish to take the test?

Act I, Scene 4

Professor (*to Crystal*) We must go this way, mustn't we?

Crystal nods

Well, I suppose so, yes.
Guardian (*holding out the fire stones*) These are the fire stones.
Professor Oh, I say...! (*He stands up and takes a stone*)
Crystal (*standing*) Father!
Professor Absolutely astounding! I have never seen alumina oxide fused with mica schist like this before. Fascinating!
Guardian Cast the stone.

The Professor does not want to let go of this unique specimen

Cast the stone.
Professor Er—you wouldn't happen to have a spare one I could take with me as a specimen——?
Guardian CAST THE STONE!

The Professor shrugs and casts the stone into the cave entrance UL. *It flares red*

Professor Amazing! That must be caused by the alumina's metamorphosis——
Guardian Pass!
Professor But Crystal——
Guardian PASS!
Professor Oh well...

The Professor picks up his bag and exits into the cave entrance UL

Guardian (*handing Crystal the other stone*) Cast the stone.

Crystal takes it, closes her eyes, crosses her fingers and throws it into the Cave entrance UL. *It flares red*

Pass.
Crystal Thank you.

Crystal picks up her bag and follows her father into the cave entrance UL. *The Guardian exits* UL

The Lights change to suggest a new landscape at the other end of the cave. Pause

The Professor enters from the cave UR. *After a pause, Crystal enters from* UR, *following her father*

Professor Ah. There you are!
Crystal Which way now, Father?
Professor Oh, let me see... this way, I think...

The Professor and Crystal exit DR

The Lights return to normal as they were at the beginning of the scene

Salmonella and Seth enter DL *and approach the cave entrance* UL. *Salmonella carries her magic bag and Seth carries the haversack*

Salmonella Aaahhh ... Hssssss!
Seth What's up?
Salmonella I was watching the Professor and his daughter at the Fiery Cave, and I don't like what I saw.
Seth What did you see, Mam?
Salmonella To get through that cave, we have to pass a test.
Seth I don't think I can pass a test.
Salmonella I don't think I can pass this one, either. Unless ... (*She reaches for her magic book*) I'll have to use some magic. (*Consulting the book*) "Spell For Changing Things" ... Hmmmm (*reading*):
"When you need to make things seem
Other than the things they've been,
Use your Magic Aerosol ..."
(*She bends down and takes the aerosol out of her bag*)
"And say the word 'Batfoldirol'
And if your spell is carefully made,
Those things will change which you have sprayed."
(*She chooses two stones from those lying around and places them* C. *She then casts the spell—not forgetting "Batfoldirol"—circling the stones as she does so*)
"Now when these stones to fire are fed,
Make them flare, and make them red!"
Yesss ... that should do nicely, Hehehehehehehe. (*She puts the stones in her bag*) Seth, come here. Stand still. Stop fidgeting. (*She slaps him*) Now listen very carefully. When we go into that cave, a man will give you a stone.
Seth Why?
Salmonella So that you can throw it into the cave.
Seth Why does he give me a stone just for me to throw it away?
Salmonella Well ... it's a kind of game.
Seth A birthday game?
Salmonella Yes—if you like, a birthday game.
Seth Ooh, goodie! What happens next?
Salmonella Well, although he wants you to throw it away——
Seth Yes?
Salmonella —it's a trick. If you throw it away, you lose!
Seth Ohh!
Salmonella Instead, if you are to win the game——
Seth Yes?
Salmonella —you must throw a different stone away.
Seth Oh.
Salmonella One that I've hidden in my bag.
Seth Yes! Yes! Yes! (*Singing*) It's a birthday game, a birthday game——
Salmonella (*thumping him*) Be quiet and listen!
Seth Yes, Mam.

Salmonella When he asks you—
Seth Who?
Salmonella The man in the cave—
Seth Yes!
Salmonella When he asks you to throw it away—
Seth Yes!
Salmonella Don't throw it away—
Seth No!
Salmonella Get rid of it—
Seth Yes! Where?
Salmonella Anywhere—your pocket—anywhere!
Seth Yes!
Salmonella Then I'll give you another stone from this bag. (*She points to the stones in her bag*)
Seth But there are ... two stones there.
Salmonella Right! One for each of us.
Seth Are you going to play, too?
Salmonella Yes.
Seth Ohhh, goodygoodygoody—
Salmonella So—I'll give you another stone, from this bag—
Seth Yes!
Salmonella And then—
Seth I put that in my pocket, too!
Salmonella No! (*She thumps him*) You throw that away.
Seth (*after a pause*) Throw it away? But you said I hadn't to throw it away!
Salmonella That was the first stone! (*Pointing into the bag*) This is the second stone. Throw this one away.
Seth (*still looking into the bag*) Mam, which of these is the second stone?
Salmonella Oh, idiot, they're *both* second stones!
Seth (*totally confused*) Both second stones?
Salmonella Listen. (*After a pause*) The man in the cave will give you a stone. Put it in your pocket—
Seth In my pocket.
Salmonella Or throw it away, get rid of it.
Seth Throw it away.
Salmonella Then you get a second stone from this bag, and you throw that one into the cave.
Seth Into the cave.
Salmonella Now, have you got that?

They look at each other for a moment. Seth is about to reply as:

The Guardian appears UL *from the cave entrance. He carries two fire stones*

Oh, never mind, just do as I say.
Seth Yes, Mam. (*To the Guardian*) Hello. I've come to play your game!
Guardian I am the Guardian of the Fiery Cave.
Seth (*after a pause*) Are you going to talk to him, Mam?

Pause

I think he wants to talk, Mam.

Pause. The Guardian folds his arms

(*Rushing to hide behind Salmonella*) I don't think I like him, Mam!

Guardian I am the Guardian of the Fiery Cave. I have been here since time began, and my sole purpose is to guard the passage through the Fiery Cave. None may pass this way, save those who satisfy the Test of the Flames. Do you know about the test?

Seth Yes. My mam's just told——

Salmonella stamps on Seth's foot

Ooowwwww! Mam!

Salmonella No.

Guardian The test is this: you must each take a fire stone and cast it into the cave. The stone will reveal whether you are good or evil. Only the good may pass. If the stone flares red, this shows you to be good, and you may proceed. If the stone flares green, then you are evil, and will be cast into the cave, to feed the fiery flames. Do you wish to take the test?

Seth No—I'm not very good at tests!

Salmonella (*thumping him*) Yes!

Guardian (*to Seth*) Take the stone.

Seth takes the stone from the Guardian

Salmonella (*whispering to Seth*) Now get rid of it.

Seth (*confused and frightened*) Now? Where?

Salmonella Anywhere! But not——

Seth throws the stone into the cave UL

—into the cave!

The stone flares red

Red? That flare was red...

Guardian Pass.

Seth Mam...?

Guardian Pass!

Seth shrugs, picks up his haversack and the magic bag containing the two false stones and starts to go into the cave entrance UL

(*To Salmonella*) Take the stone.

She realizes that the false stones are in her bag, which Seth has taken

Salmonella (*hesitating*) Erm... Er... Ssss!

Seth realizes he has the bag containing the false stones and stops, just visible inside the cave entrance

Seth (*turning back*) Mam! (*He bends down and takes a false stone from the bag*) Mam, your stone...

Salmonella acts quickly. She grabs the stone from the Guardian and throws it

Act I, Scene 5

to Seth. *Seth catches this stone, but in so doing drops his own false stone which flares red. The Guardian sees this and takes it to be the stone thrown by Salmonella*

Guardian Pass.

Salmonella joins Seth inside the cave entrance UL *and they move out of sight. Pause. The Guardian follows them into the cave* UL

The Lights change as before to suggest the new landscape at the other end of the cave

Salmonella and Seth appear from the cave UR

Seth What shall we do with this stone?
Salmonella (*cackling with delight*) Hehehehehe ... give it to me.
    If evil through and through I've been,
    No doubt this true stone will flare green!

On the last word Salmonella throws the stone in the cave UR *and there is a tremendous green flare from within the cave*

    Hehehehehe!
Seth What now, Mam?
Salmonella We must follow the Professor and his daughter of course.
Seth Why, Mam?
Salmonella (*exasperated*) Because they will lead us to the Whooperdink! (*She pauses*) Wait a minute. You've given me an idea. Why are we following them? Why don't we join them? Why not make it a party of four?
Seth A birthday party?
Salmonella Shhh? I'm thinking. If I could persuade the Professor that I too was a scientist out on an expedition——
Seth What's an exposition, Mam?
Salmonella —he might let us join him, and that would save all the fuss and bother of trying to follow him. Yesss. We'll do that. But first, I must change my clothes. Come, son!
Seth Will there be sweets at this party, Mam?

Salmonella and Seth exit DR

The Lights fade to Black-out

Scene 5

Beyond the Fiery Cave

The Lights come up as at the end of the previous scene

Crystal and the Professor enter UL. *The Professor is still talking about his experiences in the Fiery Cave*

Professor ... So I think that would explain the red flare. But I don't see how the same compounds could be made to flare green ...

Crystal Father, can we stop to eat now?
Professor Still, it's all tremendously exciting.

Crystal takes the decision to stop, and as the Professor continues talking she begins to set out a picnic

We haven't reached Urgleland yet, and we've already discovered new minerals, new rock formations, new combustible materials, all of which have never been seen before...
Crystal Do you want a cup of tea? Father?

The Professor has by now started to examine the local vegetation DL, *and has discovered a caterpillar*

Professor Come on, my beauty... that's it... come along to Daddy! (*He picks up the caterpillar*)

Salmonella and Seth enter UL. *Salmonella is now disguised as a country lady wearing her cape reversed and the collapsible witch's hat*

Salmonella stands to one side, observing and thinking how to approach the task in hand, as Seth goes over to Crystal. The Professor, unaware of the visitors, is deep in his examination of the caterpillar

Crystal (*to Seth*) Hello.
Seth Hello. What are you doing?
Crystal I'm preparing a picnic. Would you like to help?
Seth Oooh, yes please. (*He helps her lay out the picnic*)
Salmonella (*going to the Professor*) Good-afternoon! My what have we here?
Professor Oh, good-afternoon! This? Oh, a caterpillar, of the Calepteryx Splendens species.
Salmonella Really? I could do with such a specimen myself.
Professor Really? You're a naturalist too?

Salmonella nods enthusiastically

What are you studying on your trip?
Salmonella Oh... the people, animals, land... that sort of thing.
Professor But what in particular?
Salmonella Ermm—well, we thought we'd make a general survey.
Professor Let me show you some of my discoveries. (*He leads Salmonella to his bags* C *and starts to show off some of his specimens*) I found this not six metres away from a water hole; I've also found species of Lexis Lycorae, Ratus Rotundi, Elphis Elongata ... there's so much to study; did you know that in one square metre there are over two thousand five hundred different species of living organisms?
Salmonella Really? And which square metre is that?
Professor (*looking askance*) What *is* your field of interest?
Salmonella Er—that would be telling, wouldn't it?
Professor Oh, splendid! Let me guess! Herbivores? Carnivores? Fish...? Reptiles?
Salmonella Ohh yesss! Reptiles, and amphibia!

Act I, Scene 5

Professor Frogs?
Salmonella Frogs!
Professor Toads?
Salmonella Toads!
Professor Lizards?
Salmonella Lizards!
Professor Snakes?
Salmonella Snakessss!!!
Professor Oh, splendid! Tell me, would you care to join my daughter and I on our expedition? We are searching for—for—the Whooperdink!
Salmonella The Whooperdink? But I thought that it was extinct.
Professor So did I, until recently. But now I have reason to believe that one exists in Urgleland, so that is where we are going.
Salmonella Oh, ssuper! I'd love to come along! But tell me, where is Urgleland?
Professor Well... er—I think it is over in that direction. Let me see...

The Professor wanders off R *and Salmonella follows*

Crystal Where are you from?
Seth (*after a pause*) I'm not really sure.
Crystal Where are you going?
Seth (*after a pause*) I'm not really sure of that, either.
Crystal Well, what are you doing here?
Seth (*after a longer pause; about to answer as above, but just shrugging*) My mam brought me.
Crystal Which school do you go to?
Seth What's school?
Crystal Don't you know? It's a place children go to, to learn things.
Seth When do you go?
Crystal Every day—apart from weekends and holidays.
Seth It's my birthday today!
Crystal That's nice. Birthday parties are fun, aren't they?
Seth I don't know. I've never had one.
Crystal Ohh. That's a shame. (*She pauses*) My father's on an expedition, and I'm getting rather bored on my own. Would you like to come with us?
Seth What's an exposition?
Crystal Expedition! We're looking for a bird that was supposed to be extinct.
Seth I had a bird once.
Crystal Did you?
Seth It stinked too.

The Professor and Salmonella enter UR

Professor ... so we have to cross the Snowy Plains. Tell me, since your field of interest is reptiles, do you contribute to *Reptilia Monthly*?
Salmonella (*now fully carried away with herself*) Oh yes, of course!
Professor Did you read that splendid article last month about the Gastratheca?

Salmonella Read it? I wrote it! (*She is lying, of course, but in her excitement it is out before she realizes it*)
Professor *Really?* Then you must be Marcia Marcus!
Salmonella Must I? Oh, yes, that's right!
Professor Oh, this is a great privilege, Professor Marcus—or may I call you Marcia?
Salmonella Of course.
Professor (*to Crystal*) Crystal dear, let me introduce you to Professor Marcia Marcus.

Crystal and Seth stand up and Seth looks around, wondering where Professor Marcus is

(*Indicating Seth*) Who is this?
Salmonella My son, Seth.
Professor (*to Seth*) Well it's a great honour to meet your mother, Marcia.
Seth Marcia? Marcia? But she's not——

Salmonella stamps on his foot

—Mooowww!
Salmonella Here's some sweets.
Seth Ooohh, thanks, Mam.
Professor Crystal dear, Professor Marcus and her son will be joining us on our expedition—and I think we'd better be getting along.

Crystal begins to pack up the picnic

Perhaps Seth can help us with the baggage!
Salmonella Yes, of course. Seth, pick up the bags.
Seth (*doing so and noticing the jelly babies*) Oohh, sweets!

Salmonella swoops down on Seth and thumps him

Salmonella They're not for you!
Crystal (*protectively*) He wasn't to know.

Crystal and Salmonella exchange looks

Come along, Seth; I'll help you.
Professor We need those jelly babies for the Urgles. Are we ready? Then let's go. After you, Marcia.
Salmonella No, after you, er——?
Professor Uh? Ohh! I'm so sorry. Professor Percival Potterton.

They shake hands

Salmonella Then, Professor, after you!
Professor To the Whooperdink!

The Professor leads Salmonella, Crystal and Seth DR. *He stops abruptly and they all pile into each other. While the others sort themselves out the Professor moves* C *and sings*

Act I, Scene 6   19

The Whooperdink
The Whooperdink, what a wonderful bird,
Absolutely fantastic, there's no other word!
For three hundred years there's been not a sign,
But we're going to find it in a very short time.

Salmonella, Crystal and Seth move to the Professor and join in the chorus

Professor ⎫	Whooperdink, Whooperdink,
Salmonella ⎬	We're all searching for the Whooperdink
Crystal ⎬	For three hundred years there's been not a sign,
Seth ⎭	But we're going to find it in a very short time.

All prepare to exit UR *but Salmonella turns back*

Salmonella The Whooperdink is a magical bird,
In cantations of old, its name could be heard;
And now if we find it my son will be free
And the power of the Whooperdink will be all for me!

All circle round the stage while singing

Professor ⎫	Whooperdink, Whooperdink,
Salmonella ⎬	We're all searching for the Whooperdink.
Crystal ⎬	For three hundred years there's been not a sign,
Seth ⎭	But we're going to find it in a very short time.

They all exit UR

The Lights fade to Black-out

SCENE 6

The Snowy Plains

The lighting comes up to give a snowflake effect and the Snowflake Maker enters UL, *bringing with him his deckchair, snowflake machine, brochures, radio and alarm clock. He sneezes and throughout he sounds miserable and as if he has a heavy cold. Muttering to himself, he sets up his things* C *and the Lights slowly come up to full*

Snowflake Maker Snowflakes, snowflakes, snowflakes. All I ever see is snowflakes. Snowflakes and more snowflakes. I wouldn't mind if I never saw another snowflake as long as I lived. (*He pauses*) Not much chance of that, though. And however many I makes there never seems to be enough. I don't know where they all gets to. Ah well. (*He moves* DR *and makes more snowflakes*) Day after day after day. Year after year after year. I've lost track of how long I've been sitting around here making snowflakes. (*He pauses*) There must be something more to life than making snowflakes. (*He pauses*) One good thing—I'm on me own and I can please myself what I do. I can stand up, or I can sit down—but which shall I do? I'm cold either way. (*He pauses*) Oh well, time for more snowflakes. (*He makes* *more snowflakes*) Oohh, look at them. Aren't they pathetic? It's such a depressing little job, I mean, who cares, who wants snow anyway? It's so cold. (*He looks around*) All it does is make everything look the same; it's so boring. (*He pauses; sits in the deckchair and takes up his brochures*) Let's have a look at me brochures again. Aaahhhh ... look at that. Look at all that sun. There's no snow there ... there's not even any rain. Wouldn't I like to just lie down on all that—what is that? Looks like snow but it can't be. (*He reads*) Ahh ... sandy beaches. So that's what a sandy beach is. Not that I'll ever get much chance of seeing one. What a place to warm me plates o' meat. Ooohh, isn't that nice!

The Professor, Salmonella and Crystal enter UR *and put their bags down. Noticing the change in temperature they stop to put on more clothing from their bags. Seth wanders on* UR

Seth (*uncertainly; looking at his feet*) M-a-m.
Salmonella What?
Seth What's this?
Salmonella What's what?
Seth What am I standing in, Mam?
Salmonella It's snow, you fool!
Seth It's no what?
Salmonella SNOW! (*She grabs a handful and throws it at Seth*) See?
Professor Good heavens! Good Lord! What's that?
Salmonella I think there's someone over there, sitting in a striped deckchair—Ssss (*She is annoyed that she has slipped into her rhyming ways*)
Professor Absolutely fantastic—who would believe ... let's go and investigate.

All troop over to the Snowflake Maker leaving the bags where they are
Good-afternoon.
Snowflake Maker (*startled*) Uuhh? Well, blow me, where did you come from?
Crystal We've just come from the Fiery Cave——
Professor —and we're passing through here——
Salmonella —on our way to Urgleland, yess.
Snowflake Maker Would you like to stop for a chat? I haven't——
Salmonella We haven't time.
Crystal What are you doing here?
Snowflake Maker Me? I'm a Snowflake Maker.
Professor }
Crystal } (*together*) A Snowflake Maker?
Snowflake Maker It's me job; I make snowflakes.
Professor But I thought that was all to do with crystallization in the upper atmosphere ...
Crystal You look cold.
Snowflake Maker I am, me dear, I am.
Crystal What are all these brochures for?
Snowflake Maker Aahh, that's me dream, that is; a spell in the sun.
Salmonella Spell?

Act I, Scene 6

Snowflake Maker Lazing on me lilo, soaking up the sun.
Crystal But why don't you go?
Snowflake Maker I can't, can I? You see, it's me duty to stop here.
Seth How long for?
Snowflake Maker Ever and a day, son, ever and a day. I was born to this job, and I'll die in it. Like me father and his father before him.

Seth wanders away to the bags, and during the next sequence tries to sneak some jelly babies

Professor You sound as if you have a nasty cold.
Snowflake Maker I 'ave, I 'ave; I always 'ave.
Professor Have you taken anything? Pills?
Salmonella Potions?
Professor Penicillin?
Salmonella Porcupine tongues?

The Professor looks askance at her

Just a thought! Bah, enough of this; we must get on. (*She moves* UR)
Professor Yes, of course. (*He sees the snowflake machine*) Oh, I say, what is that? (*He goes to the machine*)
Salmonella (*seeing what Seth is doing*) Stop that! (*She thumps him*)

During the following, Crystal goes to the bags, speaks gently to Seth, and returns with a rug for the Snowflake Maker

Professor Fascinating. I see. He must put the water in there ... then switch ... that ... to ... there ... then this ... will make ... that ... oh I say, how absolutely splendid!
Crystal There you are. That might make you a bit warmer.
Snowflake Maker Thank you, me dear. You've got a pretty face. It's a long time since I've seen a pretty face. It's a long time since I've seen any kind of face. All I ever see is snowflakes.
Crystal And here's a clean handkerchief.
Snowflake Maker (*grabbing it and sneezing into it*) Thank you, my dear.
Salmonella (*to the Professor*) We must get on!
Professor Yes, you're right.
Crystal But can't we stay for a few more minutes and try to cheer him up?
Salmonella We've spent enough time with this old fool already. Let's go!
Professor Certainly—but I must find my bearings first. Would you care to help me?
Salmonella (*in frustration*) Ooohhh ... (*remembering she is supposed to be an enthusiastic scientist*) ... oh, yes, I'd love to help.

Salmonella and the Professor exit with the map and compass

Snowflake Maker (*to Crystal*) I'm afraid I don't much care for your mum.
Crystal She's not my mum, she's Seth's. They're friends of ours.
Snowflake Maker She doesn't look very well. Bit of a green colour to her face. She might be sickening for something.
Seth Oh no, she's always been that colour. Witch face colour is always green.

Snowflake Maker I don't know. Which face colour is always green?
Seth Yes, that's right. Witch face colour is always green.
Snowflake Maker (*puzzled, but not wishing to pursue it*) Ahh. Hmm. Well, I'd better make some more snowflakes (*He gets up and goes to the machine*) I wish I could say it's fun, but it's not.
Crystal Can't we do anything to cheer you up? (*She turns to Seth*) Seth, you try to cheer him up.

Seth goes to the Snowflake Maker and pulls funny faces, etc.

Tell him a joke. Do you know any jokes?
Seth Ooohh, yes. What goes whee—splat?
Snowflake Maker I dunno. What goes whee—splat?
Seth A caterpillar jumping off a wall without a parachute. Hehehehehe.

Seth is the only one to laugh at his joke

Crystal I know! Would you like me to sing you a song?
Snowflake Maker (*returning to sit in his deckchair*) Would you, me dear? That would be ever so nice.
Crystal It's seeing all this snow, it's reminded me of a song called "Snowflake".

The Lights return to the snowflake effect and Crystal and Seth sit at the Snowflake Maker's feet. She sings

Snowflake

Snowflake, snowflake, gently falling to the ground,
Snowflake, snowflake, softly falls without a sound.
The trees and leaves and fields are covered white with snow,
The land lies locked beneath your shell;
So light, you gleam so starry white, so bright you light the land tonight,
It's magic, and I'm lost inside your spell;
Snowflake, snowflake, gently falling to the ground,
Snowflake, snowflake, you're so good to have around.

The Lights come up to full

Snowflake Maker That was lovely, me dear; it warms the cockles of me 'eart. It reminds me of the magic snowflake. Have you heard about the magic snowflake?
Crystal No.
Snowflake Maker Shall I tell you about it?
Crystal Yes please!
Seth Oohh, yes!
Snowflake Maker Right. Well. (*He pauses*) My father told me, and his father told him, and his father before him told him about the magic snowflake. Lovely thing it must be; lovely. Not like these here snowflakes. It's bigger— much bigger—and it glistens, day and night, and it never melts. Well, that's what the story says, because, you see, no Snowflake Maker has ever seen one, no. None of us have. Oooh, but we all believes that it exists, yes we do, and we all spend our lives waiting for one to appear—because, so

Act I, Scene 6   23

the story goes, if ever a Snowflake Maker should come across a magic snowflake, then his greatest wish would be answered. It's what all of us Snowflake Makers dreams of. My father dreamed of it, and his father before him dreamed of it, and I dreams of it. I dreams and dreams of having that magic snowflake, 'cos if I had that magic snowflake I'd wish—to leave here forever! Leave this rotten cold and snow, leave it forever. 'Cos you don't know how cold it is, how miserable and lonely it gets. I'd go to the sun. That's all I wish for, all I dreams about. (*He pauses*) So, if you comes across one—I don't suppose you will, but if you do—will you please bring it to me? It's no use to you, you see, no use to anyone except a Snowflake Maker. (*He pauses*) Yes. Well, that's the story of the magic snowflake.

Salmonella and the Professor return UL

Salmonella Son, go and get the bags; we're leaving.

Seth does so

Professor Yes, get your things together, Crystal dear, we're moving on.
Snowflake Maker Already?
Crystal Never mind—we'll come back and see you sometime. I promise.
Snowflake Maker (*not really believing her*) Yes.
Professor Come along, Crystal.
Crystal Yes, Father. (*She starts towards the bags, pauses, then with just a hint of defiance she turns back to the Snowflake Maker and gives him a kiss on his cheek*) I will come back. I promise.
Snowflake Maker Thank you.

Crystal goes to collect her bag. An alarm clock rings. The Snowflake Maker stops it

Oh, 'scuse me, it's time for me programme. (*He switches his radio on and desert-island type music starts*) "Desert" ... er ... thingummy. It's me favourite. It's the only thing that really makes me feel warm. You don't know how much this means to me.

Salmonella listens to the Snowflake Maker with unusual interest, and a sly smile appears on her face. She reaches into her bag and brings out her wand

It's me only bit of comfort. It's what I live for, this programme. (*He quietly drifts off into a reverie*)

The others quietly gather their things together and tiptoe off, with Salmonella bringing up the rear. Just as she is about to exit she turns and points her wand straight at the radio. It immediately begins to crackle and hiss. Salmonella cackles delightedly and hurries off after the others

The Lights change to the snowflake effect then:

BLACK-OUT

ACT II

Scene 1

The Urgle Camp

There are ravaged strawberry plants upstage and perhaps a footprint DL

The Lights come up to give a blue effect as the Professor and Crystal enter DR

Crystal Look at these plants, Father
Professor My goodness, how amazing! (*Going to the plants*) Strawberry plants—and they're absolutely enormous. (*Peering at them*) My word! We must be getting close!
Crystal Why?
Professor Look—these strawberries; they've been ravaged. Devastated. Ravaged strawberries—well I never...
Crystal Wasn't that mentioned in the letter from Professor Wouldbegood?
Professor It certainly was. (*Looking around*) It definitely looks as though someone——
Crystal —or something——
Professor —has been eating them.
Professor ⎫
Crystal   ⎭ (*together*) The Whooperdink?
Professor Fascinating, absolutely fascinating. (*He examines the plants more closely*)

Crystal joins him

Salmonella, still in disguise, enters DR

Salmonella (*calling off*) Seth! Seth!
Seth (*off*) I'm coming, Mam.
Salmonella Son, you really are a bind; why must you always lag behind? Sss.
Seth (*off*) It's these bags, Mam; they're heavy.
Salmonella (*disgusted*) Yerghh. (*To the Professor*) Have you found something? Let me see ... (*She goes to join the Professor and Crystal*)

Seth enters DR, *carrying most of the bags, and moves towards the others. An Urgle flits across downstage. Seth sees this out of the corner of his eye*

Seth Hey! Oi! Mam! (*He turns to follow the Urgle, falls and drops the baggage. The jelly babies spill out*)
Salmonella (*coming down to Seth*) Oh, son—what have you done—sss!
Seth I saw it, Mam, I saw it. Over there. (*He points off*)
Salmonella What?
Seth (*after a pause*) I don't know—but I saw it!

Act II, Scene 1

Salmonella You fool! You're an idiot—and only idiots fall over. (*She kicks him*) Now get this lot picked up.
Crystal (*moving to join them*) What's the matter?
Salmonella My stupid son has fallen over.
Crystal (*moving to help Seth*) Is he all right?
Salmonella (*stopping her abruptly*) YESS! Leave him alone.

They look at each other for a moment

Crystal All right.
Salmonella Now, what is it your father has found?

Crystal and Salmonella return to the Professor. Seth continues to pick up the baggage

Seth (*noticing the jelly babies*) Ooohh! (*He picks one up and is about to put it into his mouth*)

An Urgle flits across, grabs the sweet from Seth's hand and dashes off

Mam! Mam! Look, Mam! I saw him again, Mam!
Salmonella (*coming down to Seth*) What?
Seth He went across there, Mam. (*He points*)

The Professor and Crystal move across to investigate

Salmonella Who did?
Seth I don't know! He pinched my jelly baby.
Salmonella (*thumping him*) How many times have I told you not to take those sweets?
Professor (*pointing to the ground* DL) LOOK!
Crystal My goodness!

The Professor and Crystal kneel down

Salmonella (*rushing over to them*) What? What? Bah—it's only a footprint! (*She makes as if to scrub it out with her foot*)
Professor }
Crystal } (*together*) NO! (*They grab her raised foot*)
Salmonella (*losing her balance and falling over*) Oohhh! Ooowww! Seth, Seth!
Seth Mam?
Salmonella Put that lot down and come and help me up.

Seth does so

Seth Mam, you said that only idiots fall down.
Salmonella Never mind that; get me up.
Seth (*struggling to bring her to her feet*) Hmph.
Salmonella Don't you laugh at me!
Seth I wasn't laughing—I was ... hmphing.
Salmonella Well, don't you hmph at me!
Professor (*still gazing intently at the footprint*) Well, well, well...
Crystal Father ... is it?

Professor I—think—it is! And look—it's got——
Crystal —a toenail missing. Father, it is! It is!
Professor }
Crystal } (*together; hugging each other*) THE WHOOPERDINK!
Professor Fantastic! Absolutely fantastic! But where is it? I wonder if it is still around?

An Urgle head peeps up from behind the strawberry plants UR

Crystal Look. Over there!

Another Urgle head appears L

Seth Mam! Look, Mam! Mamamamam!
Salmonella Yes, I see it now.
Seth I told you, I told you, na-na-ne-na-na!

Salmonella thumps Seth.

Professor Shh! (*To Crystal*) Get the jelly babies.
Seth Oohh, jelly babies!
Salmonella They're not for you.
Professor Everyone be quiet! (*He takes the bag from Crystal, takes out one jelly baby and places it* C) Now, step back.

They all do so

An Urgle suddenly dashes out, grabs the sweet and disappears

You see that? It's taken the jelly baby. (*He repeats the exercise*)

An Urgle dashes out as before, grabs the sweet and disappears

The Professor places the whole bag of jelly babies C

Seth Mam!
Salmonella Shhh!

The Chief Urgle appears UL, *wearing his chief's head dress. He picks up the bag and bows*

Chief Urgle Urgle!
Professor Ah! I see we have a language problem. Erm ...
Chief Urgle Urgle?
Professor Do you speak English?
Chief Urgle Urgle?
Professor You—speak-ee—Een-glish?
Chief Urgle Urgle?
Professor *Parlez-vous français? Sprechen sie deutsch?*
Chief Urgle Urgle?
Professor (*To himself*) Urgle ...? Urgle ...? (*Taking out a jelly baby*) Jelly baby. Jergle bergle.
Chief Urgle Jergle bergle!
Professor Yes, jergle bergle! (*Turning to his group*) Urglese! (*Looking at the Chief Urgle and pointing at the jelly baby*) Jelly baby. Jell-ee bay-bee.

Act II, Scene 1

Chief Urgle Jell-ee bay-bee?

The Professor nods

Professor (*to the rest of the group*) I think I'm getting through! (*To the Chief Urgle*) You are the Chief Urgle? Chief? Top man? Boss? He-who-is-higher-than-all-the-rest? (*He indicates the head gear of the Chief Urgle*)
Chief Urgle (*nodding*) Urgle!
Professor (*shaking the Chief Urgle's "hand"*) I'm very, very urgled to meet you! I hope you enjoy—sorry, enjergle—your jergle bergle!
Chief Urgle (*nodding and smiling*) Jergle bergle.

The rest of the Urgles creep out from the undergrowth

(*To the other Urgles*) Jell-ee bay-bee! (*To Crystal*) Jell-ee bay-bee.

Crystal nods

(*To Salmonella*) Jell-ee bay-bee.

Salmonella nods

(*To Seth*) Jell-ee bay-bee.

Seth nods, then takes the sweet and eats it. Salmonella moves as if to thump him, but then notices that the Chief Urgle is smiling, unoffended, so she restrains herself and smiles sweetly

Professor Oh, I'm so excited. This calls for a celebration.
Crystal That's a good idea. What about a song?
Professor Splendid! But I don't know whether the Urgles can sing.
Crystal Well ask them.
Professor Yes, erm ... (*He clears his throat. To the Chief Urgle*) You—erm... (*as in doh-mi-soh-doh*) urgle-urgle-urgle-urgle?
Urgles (*enthusiastically*) Urgle, urgle!
Professor Splendid—urglid! But what shall we sing together?
Crystal I know—"The Jelly Baby Song"!
Professor "The Jelly Baby Song"?
Crystal Yes. Now I'll sing it through once.

This is a suggested area for audience participation at the director's discretion. The Urgles group themselves together DR *as Crystal sings*

The Jelly Baby Song

Jergle bergle, jelly baby,
They both mean the same,
Jergle bergle, jelly baby,
It's just a different name.

Jergle bergle, jelly baby,
Won't you sing along?
Jergle bergle, jelly baby,
Our jergle baby song.

> Jergle bergle, jergle bergle,
> Jelly jelly baby;
> Jergle bergle, jergle bergle,
> Jelly jelly baby.

Professor Splendid, absolutely fantastic! Now perhaps I'd better ask them about the Whooperdink.

At the mention of the bird, there is a strong reaction from the Urgles

(*To the Chief Urgle*) Do you know? Whoo-per-dink?

All the Urgles salaam, to cries of "Whooperdink"

Seth Mam, what's going on?
Salmonella Shut up!
Crystal They seem to be bowing, Father.
Professor Yes, their actions suggest some kind of devotion to the bird, just like the book said.

The Whooperdink enters DL *and moves to the Urgles. It has a blue and purple body with yellow beak, legs and tail feathers. One of its toenails is missing*

Whooperdink Whoop.
Urgles ⎫ (*together*) ⎧ Whooperdink!
Professor ⎭ ⎩ The Whooperdink!

All the Urgles fall prostrate in front of the Whooperdink. The Professor stands transfixed. Salmonella seizes her chance and grabs the Whooperdink. The Urgles become very agitated at this

Salmonella The Whooperdink! At last it's mine! No-one can stop me now! I shall be greater than the greatest witch, wickeder than the wickedest witch, quicker than the quickest witch——
Professor You? You are a witch?
Salmonella Yes, you fools! Nothing can stop me now.
Professor Oh, we'll see about that!

The Professor and Salmonella struggle with each other over the Whooperdink

Get off!
Salmonella No!
Professor Put it down!
Salmonella No!

Salmonella shoves the Professor over on to the ground

The Whooperdink breaks free and runs off UR

Salmonella sets off in pursuit, but the Professor grabs her leg; she struggles free and sets off again in pursuit

Come back! Come back!

Salmonella exits UR

Seth Mam ...!

Act II, Scene 1

Immediately the Urgles seize Seth, who is still carrying the bags, and Crystal and hold them at dagger point

Professor Oh dear, this is absolutely dreadful! Crystal, are you all right?
Chief Urgle Urgle!
Professor Look, I'm dreadfully sorry—I mean, urgally urgle——
Chief Urgle (*imposingly*) Urgle ... (*pointing at the Professor*) ... urgle Whooperdink ... (*pointing off* UR) ... urgle Whooperdink urgle ... (*pointing at the ground in front of him*) ... urgle ... (*He points at the hostages and makes a throat-cutting gesture and noise*)
Professor Oh dear, oh dear. (*To Seth and Crystal*) I think he's saying that I've got to go and fetch the Whooperdink back here, or ... (*he points to the hostages and repeats the Chief Urgle's noise and gesture*)

The Chief Urgle repeats the throat-cutting noise and gesture

Salmonella enters UR, *suitably dishevelled and out of breath*

Professor Where's the Whooperdink?
Salmonella It disappeared among the strawberry plants. I couldn't get through, oh what shall I do? Sss.
Professor You've done enough already. Look.
Salmonella What's happened?
Professor They're being held as hostages, and unless we get the Whooperdink back, they're going to ... (*he repeats the throat-cutting noise and gesture*)

Salmonella repeats the throat-cutting noise and gesture as does the Chief Urgle

(*Leading Salmonella to one side*) Listen, are you really a witch?
Salmonella Of course I am!
Professor Well, if you're a witch, can't you do something—cast a spell, for instance?
Salmonella Of course I could—but all my magic devices are in my bag!

Salmonella moves towards Seth who is carrying the bag, but the Urgles drive her back

Bah! (*To the Professor*) Can't you do something?
Professor Well ... I could mix my nitrate and potash solution ...
Salmonella What would that do?
Professor Well, judging from previous experience, it ought to make a loud bang.
Salmonella Excellent!
Professor But——
Salmonella What?
Professor —the ingredients are in my bag, which your son is also carrying.
Salmonella Oooohhh!
Professor I think we have to go and find the Whooperdink.
Salmonella Yes, the choices do seem few indeed, since we can't get the bags we need. Sss.
Professor (*to the Chief Urgle*) Urgle ... (*indicating himself and Salmonella*)

... urgle Whooperdink ... (*pointing in the direction of departed Whooperdink*) ... and return urgle ... (*pointing at the ground in front of him*)

The Chief Urgle produces a chalice of jam, which he gives to the Professor

Now, what's this? Oh, I say, it's jam ... mmmm ... strawberry, definitely, ... and made quite recently too.
Chief Urgle (*indicating the jam*) Urgle urgle Whooperdink ... slurp slurp slurp (*He goes through the motions of slurping up the jam*)
Professor Of course—(*to Salmonella*) jam is the Whooperdink's favourite food!
Salmonella We'd better go, or we'll never catch it.
Professor Yes, you're right. It'll soon be dark. Don't worry, Crystal, I'll soon be back.
Salmonella I'll show you the way it went.

Salmonella and the Professor exit UR

Seth Mam ...!
Crystal Don't worry, Seth, I'm sure she'll be back. Anyway, I'm here with you, too. We'll help each other, won't we?

The Urgles indicate to the hostages that they want them to move off DL

Crystal I'll help carry your bags. (*As she bends down, she notices one of the Whooperdink's feathers*) Oh look, one of the Whooperdink's feathers. It must have fallen in the struggle. (*She picks it up and takes it with her*)

Crystal, Seth and the Urgles exit

Fade to Black-out

SCENE 2

The Snowy Plains

The Lights come up to give a snowflake effect on the Snowflake Maker who is sitting in his deckchair C, *reading one of his brochures*

Snowflake Maker "... Pria da Rocha has excellent sandy beaches, divided in places by strangely-shaped rocks. There is a long promenade above the beach, where you can gaze down on the golden-yellow sand, the red rocks and a sapphire sea ..."

The Lights come up to full

The Whooperdink enters UR, *and during the following sequence, flaps to and fro, but mainly around the Snowflake Maker*

Whooperdink Whoop! Whoop!
Snowflake Maker My goodness me! What in the world ...
Whooperdink Please whoop, please whoop, you must help me.
Snowflake Maker 'Ere, you got hiccups?

Act II, Scene 2 31

Whooperdink No—oh please can you help me?
Snowflake Maker 'Cos if you have I'm not surprised, all that dashing about.
Whooperdink I need to get away from the wicked witch! Whoop!
Snowflake Maker There you go again! You should take something for that.
Whooperdink Whoop, please!
Snowflake Maker Have you tried holding your breath? I'm told that's very good——
Whooperdink Please can you help me?
Snowflake Maker —though not if you hold it for too long, of course.
Whooperdink PLEASE!
Snowflake Maker Sorry. What can I do for you?
Whooperdink The wicked witch is following me, I'm hungry and whoop frightened, whoop. Can you help me to get away?
Snowflake Maker 'Ere. You haven't got a magic snowflake with you, have you?
Whooperdink A magic snowflake?
Snowflake Maker Yes. Well?
Whooperdink Whoop, no, I haven't. I'm sorry.
Snowflake Maker Ah well, I didn't think you would have. No-one ever has.
Whooperdink Is there somewhere I can hide?
Snowflake Maker (*laughing*) Hide? Here? Where? You tell me. It's all the same! Boring snow.
Whooperdink But—whoop—what about the wicked witch?
Snowflake Maker Witch? There's no witch around here. All we have round here is snowflakes. I'm sick of the sight of snowflakes. That's all I ever see is snowflakes——
Whooperdink Oooohh, whoop!

The Whooperdink rushes off UL *in frustration*

Snowflake Maker (*oblivious to the Whooperdink exit*)—until recently, that is. Just lately it's been nothing but people rushing forward, rushing back, rushing here, rushing there. Take that last lot, for instance. They weren't very interested in snowflakes—not as I blames 'em. All they tried to do was tell silly jokes to try to cheer me up. (*Pause*) The girl was nice, though. (*Pause*) Anyway, getting back to your problem—(*he looks around for the Whooperdink and realizes it has gone*) Ohh. Typical. Nobody ever stops to pass the time of day these days. Ah well ... (*He returns to his brochures*)

The Professor and Salmonella enter UR *following the Whooperdink's footprints in the snow, the Professor leading the way, looking through his magnifying glass. He follows footprints round the Snowflake Maker's deckchair*

Professor ... its tracks are very fresh here ... my goodness—there's a new set of tracks ... footprints ...! And they look very similar to—er—mine! (*His sight comes to rest on the Snowflake Maker's feet and he follows them up with his glass until face to face with the Snowflake Maker's brochure*) Erm—excuse me.
Snowflake Maker Ahh. You again.

Professor Yes——
Salmonella (*shoving the Professor aside*) Where's the Whooperdink?
Snowflake Maker The——
Salmonella Where is it?
Snowflake Maker What's——?
Professor It must have been this way——
Salmonella We followed the tracks——
Professor Right up to here——
Salmonella So we know it's been here——
Professor It must have been, yes.
Salmonella So where is it?
Professor Have you seen it?
Salmonella You must have seen it!
Professor Have you hidden it?
Salmonella You must have hidden it!
Snowflake Maker One question——
Salmonella —at a time! I know, I know.
Snowflake Maker 'Ere. You don't happen to have a magic snowflake with you, do you?
Professor Magic snowflake?
Salmonella (*to the Snowflake Maker*) Bah! Stop rambling and listen!
Snowflake Maker No, I didn't suppose you would have. Never mind.

The Snowflake Maker picks up his brochures again to resume reading and Salmonella knocks them out of his grasp

'Ere!
Salmonella Where—is—it? The Whooperdink!
Snowflake Maker (*after a pause*) A funny bird, like, is it?
Salmonella ⎫
Professor ⎭ (*together*) Yes!
Snowflake Maker Bluey-purple sort of colour?
Salmonella ⎫
Professor ⎭ (*together*) Yes, yes!
Snowflake Maker Yellowy feathers, an' that?
Salmonella ⎫
Professor ⎭ (*together*) Yes, yes, yes!
Snowflake Maker (*after a pause*) I dunno.
Salmonella AAARGHHH! (*In a rage she grabs the brochure, tries to rip it in half, fails, so throws it on the ground and leaps and stamps upon it in a fair old temper*)
Professor Marcia—the tracks—they lead this way. Come on.

The Professor exits UL. *Salmonella has a final stamp on the brochure, kicks it towards the Snowflake Maker and hurries off after the Professor*

Snowflake Maker And good riddance. Look at me brochure. One of me few pleasures in life, and look what happens. The green-faced old goat.

Pause. The Lights fade to the snowflake effect

Act II, Scene 3   33

I wonder what happened to the other two? Them young 'uns. What was she called? Crystal. Yeah, Crystal. Nice face ... nice name. Reminds me of the Magic Snowflake ... Crystal ...

As the Snowflake Maker drifts off into another reverie, the Lights fade to Black-out

Scene 3

The Urgle Camp. Night

There is a cage C *in which Seth and Crystal are locked and bound. In the bottom of the cage is the Whooperdink feather. (The feather should be lightly coated with fluorescent paint so that it will glow later in the scene)*

The stage is in total darkness. Suddenly we hear Seth's plaintive voice

Seth M-a-m ...!
Crystal Don't worry, Seth, I'm here.

Slowly, a dim, general lighting comes up with a spotlight on Seth and Crystal

Seth I don't like the dark
Crystal Never mind, it'll soon be light.

Pause

Seth It's been a rotten birthday.
Crystal Why does your mother keep hitting you?
Seth We-ll, she's not as bad as she used to be. I remember in the old days, when she got really annoyed she used to hit me with her broomstick.
Crystal My father would never hit me. It must be awful to have a mother like that. But she didn't do it often, did she?
Seth No—no—when she was asleep she didn't do it at all.
Crystal Why does she hit you so much?
Seth I dunno. 'Cos I'm stupid, I suppose.
Crystal Oh, it's so sad. You can't help it, can you?

Seth shrugs. Silence. In the darkness, the feather starts to glow, and Seth notices it

Seth Look.
Crystal (*picking up the feather*) It seems to be glowing. Do you like it?
Seth Yes. It's very ...
Crystal Pretty?
Seth Yes, pretty. (*Looking at Crystal*) Very pretty.
Crystal (*handing the feather to Seth*) Here. Take it. It's my birthday present to you.
Seth Ooohh. Thank you.

Pause

Crystal You're such a nice person, really; yet no-one can be bothered with you. Do you have any friends?

Seth What's a friend?
Crystal Well, it's someone you can talk to; someone who listens. Someone you like to be with. (*She pauses*) And now your mum and my dad have left us ... and I don't know when they'll be coming back ... if they come back at all.
Seth I think I'd like a friend.
Crystal (*starting to cry*) Oh, Seth. Sad, simple Seth. (*She cries*)
Seth Oh, don't cry, please don't cry. No.

Seth wipes Crystal's tears away with the feather. Immediately the eerie forest sounds and the last two lines of the curse from Act I, Scene 2, come floating over the air

Voice   "A whoop, a cry, a brush so light—
              Together these will make him bright."

The eerie forest sounds stop and Seth appears to undergo some change as clearly the spell is lifted. The feather stops glowing. As soon as the transformation is complete, Seth notices something lying on the ground at Crystal's feet

Seth Look. (*He bends down and picks up the object*)
Crystal It's like a snowflake.
Seth But it's too large.
Crystal And it's not melting in your hand.
Seth It must be—a magic snowflake! Remember? It's what the Snowflake Maker told us about.
Crystal I'm sure you're right. But how?
Seth I don't know. You were crying, and ... that's it! Your tears must have made it!
Crystal But why?
Seth You were crying ... because you felt sorry for me. Perhaps when people cry for the right reasons ...
Crystal Seth—you've changed.
Seth Yes ... I do feel different, somehow.
Crystal But you can think—you're not stupid any more. What's happened to you?
Seth I'm not sure. I remember—I remember a curse. Yes, that's it! (*He rummages in the magic bag and finds the spell book*) Yes, here it is. (*Reading*)
        "This curse shall last for twenty years;
            It shall begin and end in tears."
You were crying; they were your tears.
        "For what had gone is here again;
            Its magic may give him a brain."
Crystal The Whooperdink had gone. Everyone thought it was extinct. But it isn't.
Seth And its magic—must be in its feathers!
Crystal Look. The feather has stopped glowing.
Seth The magic has been used! (*Eagerly, reading on*)
        "A whoop, a cry, a brush so light."

Act II, Scene 3

"A whoop"—the Whooperdink; "a cry"—your tears; "a brush so light" ...
Crystal "A brush so light" ...?
Seth The feather! I used it to brush away your tears!
Crystal That's right! (*Overjoyed*) Oh, Seth!
Seth (*very business-like*) Right. If I have a brain now, let's see if I can put it to good use. How do we get out of here?
Crystal What about the magic snowflake?
Seth Yes! No! Don't you remember—only a Snowflake Maker can use it! If we could get to the Snowflake Maker, then maybe he would use it to help us get my mum, your dad and the Whooperdink back.
Crystal That's a good idea—but first we've got to get out of this cage.
Seth Hmm. (*He settles himself to think*) What's in your father's bag?
Crystal Oh, specimens, chemicals—
Seth What are chemicals?
Crystal Oh, they—er—they—dissolve things! That's it! Oh, you are clever, Seth! (*She rummages in her father's bag and produces a bottle of acid*) This will burn through our ropes and the chain on the door! (*She starts to unscrew the acid lid*)
Seth Wait a minute. If we escape, the Urgles will chase us and probably catch us again. (*After a pause, slowly*) It would be better if we could persuade the Urgles to come with us to the Snowflake Maker.
Crystal You're right! But how do we do that?
Seth I know! If we show them that we *could* have escaped, but didn't, they might trust us.
Crystal Oh, Seth, it's worth a try.

Seth takes the acid, and goes to the cage door

Seth (*shouting*) Urgle! Urgle! Urgle!

Soon a batch of Urgles, including the Chief Urgle, appear DL

Chief Urgle Urgle?
Seth Urgle.

Seth demonstrates the power of the acid—first on his own bindings, and then on the door chain. The chain falls to the floor and the cage door swings open. The Urgles stand amazed

Chief Urgle Urgle?
Seth We (*he points to himself and Crystal*)—go (*he points away*)—bring—Whooperdink here (*he points to the ground. He then repeats this, trying his version of pidgin Urglese*) Wergle—gergle—brergle—Whooperdink—hergle.
Chief Urgle (*repeating the words and the actions*) Wergle—gergle—brergle—Whooperdink—hergle?

Seth and Crystal nod. The Chief Urgle consults his guards, then returns to Seth and Crystal

(*Nodding*) Urgle. (*Indicating one guard*) Urgle urgle. (*indicating a second guard*) urgle urgle (*pointing away*) urgle (*pointing at Seth and Crystal*) urgle urgle.

Seth (*to Crystal*) I think it's OK, but he wants these two guards to come with us. (*To the Chief Urgle; pointing at the first guard*) Urgle (*pointing at the second guard*) urgle urgle (*pointing away*) urgle (*pointing at himself and Crystal*) urgle urgle?

Chief Urgle (*nodding*) Urgle!

Seth and Crystal, their bonds untied, pick up their bags and leave the cage. The Lights come up to full

Seth (*to Crystal*) Ready?

Crystal Ready. Look—here comes the dawn.

Seth and Crystal smile at each other and exit UR, *with their escort*

The Lights fade to Black-out

SCENE 4

Outside the Fiery Cave

The Lights come up to suggest the landscape on the other side of the cave

The Guardian enters from the cave entrance UR. *The Whooperdink dashes in* DR *and is about to run into the cave*

Guardian HALT! Who dares come into my cave like this?

Whooperdink Whoop, whoop, Whooperdink; whoo, whoo, I'm so hungry, whoop, and (*he gulps*) whoop, somebody's following me (*he gulps*) whoop, the wicked witch, whoop, won't you help me?

Guardian I am the Guardian of the Fiery Cave. I have been here since time began——

Whooperdink Whoop, whoop, please let me hide in there, just for a minute.

Guardian —and my sole purpose is to guard the passage through the Fiery Cave——

Whooperdink Whoop, whoop, and I'm so hungry. Do you have any food, any jam, whoop, strawberry jam?

Guardian None may pass this way——

Whooperdink I'll hide behind you, then, shall I? (*He gulps*) Will you let me h-h-hide behind you? (*He gulps*)

Guardian —save those who satisfy the Test of the Flames.

Whooperdink Oh, whoop, oh, whoop. (*He tries to run past the Guardian on the Guardian's left-hand side*)

Guardian (*raising his cloaked arm to block the way*) NO!

The Whooperdink recoils, looks at the Guardian and tries to get past the Guardian's right-hand side, with the same result

NO!

Act II, Scene 4

The Guardian stands with his arms outstretched. The Whooperdink stares hard at the Guardian, then looks behind, repeats the look both ways, and, thoroughly exhausted and upset, sinks to the ground at the Guardian's feet, so that he is hidden behind a rock close to the cave entrance

The Guardian looks down at the Whooperdink, then retires into the cave UR

Whooperdink *(sobbing and whooping)* Whoop. *(He gulps)* Whoop. *(He gulps)* I—I—I don't know what to do. I can't go much further. *(He gulps)* I'm so tired and hungry, *(he gulps)* whoop, whoop, if only I could have some jam, whoop, oh for some strawberry jam ... *(He sobs quietly)*

The Professor and Salmonella enter DR, *following the tracks through a magnifying glass*

Salmonella Are we still on the right track?
Professor Yes ... the trail is very fresh here *(He looks up)* Oh, there's that cave!

Neither the Professor or Salmonella can see the Whooperdink hidden behind the rock

Salmonella Ssss!
Professor Yes, with those marvellous stones. *(Moving towards the cave)* I wonder if——
Salmonella *(grabbing the Professor)* NO! I can't—er, we mustn't go back there.
Professor But why ever not? It's a fascinating cave, and there are some fabulous felspar formations—and the Whooperdink might be in there.
Salmonella Yes ...
Professor Come on, then.
Salmonella *(pulling back)* No!
Professor What's the matter? Are you afraid?
Salmonella *(on her dignity)* Me? Salmonella? The greatest witch!?
Professor I don't believe you're a witch at all.
Salmonella Of course I am! And when I get the Whooperdink, I shall keep it and its powers forever!
Professor Oh no you won't!
Salmonella Oh yes I will!
Professor Oh no you won't *(etc., at director's discretion)* If you're a witch, prove it. Show me some magic.
Salmonella I can't, curse you. Stupid Seth still has my magic bag. But I can show you ... *(She reverses her cloak revealing the witch's side which she wears from now on, and flips out the dome of her country hat, which turns it back into a witch's hat)* See!
Professor Oh. Hmm...
Salmonella Listen!

They listen, and hear whooping and sobbing noises coming from the cave area

Whooperdink I'm so tired, whoop, *(he gulps)* and so hungry ...
Salmonella *(to the Professor)* Hungry!

Whooperdink If only I had some strawberry jam ...
Salmonella (*whispering to the Professor*) Jam! Jam! (*She points to the Professor's pocket, which contains the chalice of jam*)
Professor (*absorbed*) What? (*He feels in his pocket*) Oh, yes, jam! (*He takes out the chalice of jam*) What shall we do with it? Shall I take it in to the Whooperdink?
Salmonella No, you fool!
Professor But I may be able to coax the poor thing out.
Salmonella (*contemptuously*) That won't work. We need to set a trap.
Professor A trap? I don't believe in trapping things.
Salmonella Hah! What about all your specimens, trapped in tubes?

The Professor, for once, is silent. Salmonella grabs the chalice, takes off the lid, and sets the chalice down outside the cave entrance

Stand there, and when the Whooperdink appears, grab it!

They stand one on either side of the cave entrance. The Whooperdink's sobs turn to sniffs as it picks up the scent of the jam

Whooperdink Jam ...? Strawberry jam ...? (*He follows his nose out from behind the rock, sees the jam and pounces on it*) Slurp, slurp ... mmmmmmmmmmmmm ...!

Salmonella and the Professor stand momentarily transfixed at this scene. Just as Salmonella is about to pounce, the Professor speaks

Professor (*unable to contain himself*) Fascinating, absolutely fascinating!

The Whooperdink hears this, realizes the danger, and bolts forward just as Salmonella dives for him. The Whooperdink rushes into the audience and Salmonella ends up in a heap on the floor

Salmonella (*to the Professor*) You fool!

Salmonella quickly gets to her feet and sets off in pursuit of the Whooperdink. The chase continues round the auditorium and in among the audience, whilst the Professor stands C, watching and fretting—and possibly ad libbing to encourage audience response

Professor Oh dear, what shall I do ...? I don't want to hurt it or frighten it ... but I must save Crystal ... Oh dear oh dear ... what shall I do?

Eventually the Professor intercepts the Whooperdink and he is caught

Salmonella (*holding the Whooperdink*) At last, at last!
Professor Be careful don't hurt it.
Salmonella (*to the Whooperdink*) Where are your magic powers? (*Shaking the Whooperdink*) Where are they?
Whooperdink (*frightened*) Whoop, whoop ...
Professor (*interceding*) Stop it. Stop it! You're hurting it!
Salmonella (*seeing she is getting nowhere and stopping*) All right. All right! But when we get back to Urgleland, I'll find out then, you understand?
Professor I understand. Let's go.

Act II, Scene 5   39

The Professor puts his arm protectively around the Whooperdink and leads him out DR, *muttering words of comfort. Salmonella follows them*

(*As they go*) There we are, Whoopy, you're all right now, don't let that nasty witch frighten you ...

The Lights fade to Black-out

SCENE 5

The Snowy Plains

The snowflake lighting effect comes up on the Snowflake Maker who is sitting in his deckchair C, *reading his brochures*

Crystal, Seth and the Urgles enter DR

Crystal There he is.

The Lights come up to full

The Snowflake Maker. (*To the Snowflake Maker*) Hello!
Snowflake Maker My goodness me! Well, well, well, if it isn't our Crystal and——
Crystal Seth.
Snowflake Maker Seth, yes. But I don't recognize your other friends. They're not Mum and Dad in disguise, are they?
Crystal (*smiling*) No. We've brought you something. Look (*She shows him the magic snowflake*)
Snowflake Maker Blimey! (*He stands, and is mesmerized by it*) I can't believe me eyes. It's a magic snowflake. Is it really? I never thought I'd see the day—can I?
Crystal Of course. (*She hands it to him*)
Snowflake Maker Oh my giddy aunt ... ain't it beautiful. I can't believe it! At last I can have me wish. Oh thank you, thank you, me dear. (*He stands up and hugs and kisses Crystal*)
Crystal Well it was Seth who found it really.
Snowflake Maker (*likewise hugging and kissing Seth*) Oh thank you, thank you! Oh, I'm so excited. Where shall I go? (*He reaches for a brochure*) Which sandy beach shall I choose?
Crystal Well ... we were wondering ...
Snowflake Maker Yes? You know somewhere nice? I'll go there. If you recommend it, it must be good.
Crystal No, listen, please.
Snowflake Maker What?
Crystal (*after a pause*) My dad and his mum have gone to find the Whooperdink, and we're trying to find them. Is there any chance you might use this magic snowflake to bring them all back?
Snowflake Maker What? (*To Seth*) Your mum? That green-faced old goat? No chance.

Crystal Please.
Snowflake Maker NO.
Seth Please.
Snowflake Maker Never in a million years, son. Never in a million, billion, trillion years! You don't know how long I've waited for this. I owes it to all Snowflake Makers, my father——
Crystal But you don't know how much my father means to me. I want him back safe and sound. I love him.
Snowflake Maker (*softening*) Yes, but...
Seth And there's my mum, too.
Snowflake Maker That grizzly green-faced grouser! No, me mind's made up! (*He is about to throw the magic snowflake*)

The Professor, the Whooperdink and Salmonella enter UL

Professor Crystal!
Crystal (*running to the Professor and hugging him*) Dad, oh Dad! I'm so glad you're safe!
Salmonella Seth, is that you?
Seth It is, yes.
Salmonella Seth? You sound different.
Seth I'm not stupid any more, Mum. The spell has been broken.
Salmonella What is four times four?
Seth Sixteen.
Salmonella What do you like to eat?
Seth Swee—— Chocolates.
Salmonella How many p's in poppy?
Seth Three, Mum.
Salmonella Ha—there's only—oh yes, three. You're right. You have changed. How?
Seth It's a long story, Mum.
Salmonella I'm waiting.
Seth Well, remember the last lines of the curse—"A whoop, a cry"?
Salmonella Yes.
Seth The whoop was the Whooperdink's magic, and the cry——

Seth holds out his hand to Crystal who moves towards him

—the cry was Crystal's tears.
Salmonella Crysssstal! Yes, go on.
Seth And "the brush so light"—that was a feather Crystal gave me as my birthday present. I used it to brush away her tears.
Salmonella A feather?
Seth Yes, the Whooperdink's feathers are magic——
Crystal (*aghast*) SETH!
Salmonella Aha!

The secret is out, and, whilst Seth holds his head in shame and horror, Salmonella grabs the Whooperdink once again

Now, at last, I shall be the greatest witch! All powerful! I shall turn this

Act II, Scene 5

land of snow into freezing ice! You think you've been cold? You don't know what cold is, yet! Ssssss! (*To the Professor*) You. You interfering old intellectual, with your precious rocks. I shall turn you into solid rock, and you shall stay buried beneath the ice for ever and ever! (*To Seth*) I've had to put up with your stupidity for twenty years. And now that the curse is lifted, you're none the wiser! I can see what you feel for her. You think her spell over you is stronger than any of mine? Ha! Well, think again! I could have made you great, now that the curse has gone. You could have flown with me, been my greatest familiar! But now—since you love her, you can stay with her and share her fate! (*To Crystal*) As for you... you will never touch or see him again. Your heart will be the start, and from there you will turn into a solid lump of ice. You will go colder and colder, and as you freeze, your feet will stick to the ground and you will never be heard of or seen again! Now, with this feather——(*She reaches for one of the Whooperdink's feathers*)
Snowflake Maker NO!

The Snowflake Maker throws the magic snowflake at the witch. She is showered in magic snow, and freezes instantly. There is a stunned silence

Professor What happened?
Crystal You used it! You did it after all! You used your only chance to stop the witch.
Snowflake Maker Yes.

Crystal runs to the Snowflake Maker and hugs and kisses him. Seth does likewise

Crystal But what about you now? You've stopped the witch, and she can't harm the Whooperdink, and that's marvellous. But you've lost your chance to get away.
Snowflake Maker Yes. Yes, I have, haven't I?
Crystal Oh, what a shame. You've waited such a long time, (*she starts to cry*) dreamed about it for so long. (*She cries*)
Snowflake Maker I don't care.
Crystal What?
Snowflake Maker Really, it doesn't matter now. I've seen it, I've held it, and I've used it. Used it to help you. (*He sniffs*) And do you know, I've never felt happier!
Seth But your dreams, the sunshine...?
Snowflake Maker Well, I've still got me dreams, ain't I? And me brochures. But for once in my life I've been able to do something useful, to help somebody. And no sun could make me feel warmer inside than I am now.
Crystal (*crying*) Oh, Mr Snowflake Maker.

Crystal and the Snowflake Maker have a good cry together

Professor My goodness! Good gracious! (*He bends down to the feet of the Snowflake Maker and Crystal*) Whatever can these be?
Seth (*bending down*) Your tears. They've become——

Seth
Crystal } *(together)* — magic snowflakes!
Snowflake Maker Magic snowflakes!
Seth One ... two ... three. *(To the Snowflake Maker)* Look. Take them, they're yours.
Snowflake Maker But how? Why?
Seth I don't really know — but I think it's something to do with crying for the right reasons.
Professor Well, whatever the reason, Mr Snowflake Maker has three more of these ...
Crystal Magic snowflakes!
Professor Yes, three more magic snowflakes to use. What are you going to do with them?

The Urgles step forward, and indicate that they would like their Whooperdink back

1st Urgle Urgle Whooperdink urgle!
2nd Urgle Urgle!
Professor Oh. I think they want their Whooperdink back. *(To the 1st Urgle)* Urgle Whooperdink urgle?
1st Urgle
2nd Urgle } *(together, nodding)* Urgle.
Crystal Well, we did promise, didn't we?
Seth Yes, we did.
Professor Yes, of course. *(After a pause)* Only ...
Crystal What?
Professor Well, we've come all this way on the quest for the Whooperdink, and here it is. And now they're going to take it away from me, and I'll probably never see it again. Oh, botheration! So near, and yet so far. If only I had some evidence. A photograph. But I haven't brought my camera. Oh, I wish I had a camera!
Snowflake Maker Then you shall have one.
Professor But——
Snowflake Maker I can wish one for you!
Crystal Would you really?
Snowflake Maker Of course I would. Oooh, I haven't had so much fun in — in — ever! Stand back! *(He puts two magic snowflakes down, and prepares to throw the third)*
Professor Erm ... could you make it a Polaroid 2000, please?
Snowflake Maker One Polaroid 2000 coming up!
Professor Thank you so much.

The Snowflake Maker throws the magic snowflake at the Professor's bag

Crystal *(fetching the bag)* Look in the bag, Father.
Professor Oooh, isn't this exciting. I can hardly bear to look. *(He looks in the bag; there is a squeal of delight)* It is, it is! A Polaroid 2000! Splendid, absolutely! *(To Crystal)* Would you, please ... ?

Act II, Scene 5   43

The Professor gives the camera to Crystal and he poses alongside the Whooperdink. Crystal takes a photograph and everyone gathers around to look at it. (It is possible to load a Polaroid 2000 with a previously-taken photograph, thus allowing for really "instant" photographs.) The Urgles "ask" to see it, and indicate that they would like a photograph taken, too. Crystal takes a photograph of the Professor, the Whooperdink and the two Urgles

Crystal Smile! Urgle!

The Urgles are given their photograph, with which they are extremely pleased, and they exit UL *with their photograph and the Whooperdink*

The Professor sits down and gazes rapturously at his photograph

You still have a magic snowflake left. You still have the chance to make your dreams come true.
Snowflake Maker I still have two left. I only need one for my wish. What about you? Don't you have a wish?
Crystal (*thoughtfully*) Ye-es, but (*looking at Seth*) I was hoping it would come true without the help of magic. (*Still looking at Seth, but speaking to the Snowflake Maker*) What about Seth?
Snowflake Maker Well?
Seth (*looking at Crystal*) It's true, I do have one great wish, but ...
Crystal Maybe ours is the same wish, Seth. (*She holds out her hand to Seth*)
Seth (*taking her hand*) Maybe it is.

Crystal and Seth gaze into each other's eyes

Snowflake Maker Well, that saves a magic snowflake.
Crystal But don't forget your wish—to leave here for a place in the sun.
Snowflake Maker You know, I'm not sure I want to leave here after all.
Crystal }
Seth } (*together*) What?
Snowflake Maker We-ell ... things have picked up here lately, it's really been quite lively ... and all things considered, I think I'd miss it. And then, I have a duty, you know, to make all this snow; I mean, not everybody can be a snowflake maker. (*He pauses*) Now what I really would like is a little spell off ...
Seth Spell?
Snowflake Maker Yes, say a fortnight's holiday, once a year. Yes, that would do nicely.
Seth In that case, why don't you use a magic snowflake to release my mother from her spell, so that she could do your job while you're away?
Crystal What a good idea.
Seth It'll be her punishment for the way she's behaved.
Crystal And to stop her behaving like that in the future, can you wish away her witching powers and make her a good, simple mortal like everyone else?
Seth Er—Crystal.
Crystal Yes, Seth?
Seth Please—not simple!

Crystal Oh dear, of course not!
Snowflake Maker Right. Here we go.

The Snowflake Maker closes his eyes tight shut, concentrates, and throws the magic snowflake at Salmonella. She unfreezes, and from here on is a typically nice mum—named Marcia, though understandably, the rest are cautious at first

Seth Hello, Mum.
Marcia Hello, Seth. What's happened? Gosh my arms are stiff.
Seth Er—you've probably been standing in a draught.
Marcia My word, it's chilly. What are we doing here?
Seth Ah, Mum, let me introduce you. The Snowflake Maker.
Marcia (*going and shaking hands*) Very pleased to meet you.
Seth Professor Percival Potterton.
Marcia (*going and shaking hands*) How do you do.
Seth And—Crystal.
Marcia Crystal...

The others wait with bated breath

What a nice name. And such a pretty face!
Seth Mum, Mr Snowflake Maker would like to take a holiday each year, just for two weeks. Would you mind standing in for him while he's away?
Marcia Well... not so long as he gives me something warm to stand in.

They all laugh and the atmosphere relaxes

Professor Oh, it really is a pleasure to know you now, Marcia!
Marcia (*to the Snowflake Maker*) Will I be able to use that machine?
Snowflake Maker Yes of course, me dear. I'll show you.

The Snowflake Maker and Marcia go to the snowflake machine DR *to make snowflakes. He calls over the Professor, Seth and Crystal and they all have a try*

Right. Hows about you all coming back with me to my place? We can all have a nice hot chocolate to celebrate.
Seth Chocolate!
Snowflake Maker And you can all help me to decide where I should go for my holidays.
All What a good idea, splendid, etc.
Seth Just a minute. You still have one magic snowflake left. (*Going and picking it up from beside the deckchair*) Here.
Snowflake Maker The last magic snowflake. What shall I do with it? (*He pauses*) I know, I know! We'll use it for all the children here tonight. (*To the children*) Go on, make your own very special wish. And, if it's a good one, and you keep it a secret, may—it—come—true!

The Snowflake Maker throws the magic snowflake, in a sweeping motion, over the audience, who are showered by "magic snow"

Professor Well, that's absolutely splendid, absolutely fantastic! I've never seen anything like it; I must say——

Crystal Oh, Father!
Professor Yes. Er—I must say I'm ready for that chocolate. How about you, Marcia? (*He offers his arm*)
Marcia (*taking his arm*) I'd be delighted—Percival.

They start to move, arm in arm, followed by Seth and Crystal, arm in arm. The Snowflake Maker follows

Snowflake Maker I understand that Majorca is very pleasant this time of year...

Everyone exits

The Lights fade to—
        BLACK-OUT

FURNITURE AND PROPERTY LIST

Each scene can be set as elaborately or as sparsely as required. The play can be performed in the round, against black curtains, or within a traditional box set. Accordingly, the furniture and properties listed below are the minimum required.

ACT I

Scene 1

On stage: Laboratory bench. *On it:* glassware, bottle marked "nitrate", bottle marked "potash", bottle marked "sulphuric acid", glass flask with toenail inside, specimen jars, cloth
Bookshelf L *On it:* reference book, etc.

Off stage: 2 travel bags (**Professor** and **Crystal**)
Magnifying glass (**Professor**)
Mosquito net (**Crystal**)
Compass (**Professor**)
Cardigan (**Crystal**)
Specimen Jars (**Professor**)
Sunhats (**Crystal**)
Retort (**Professor**)
Rug (**Crystal**)
Tripod (**Professor**)
Thermos Flask (**Crystal**)
Sextant (**Professor**)
Sunglasses (**Crystal**)
Geological hammer (**Professor**)
Galoshes (**Crystal**)

Personal: Crystal: letter/map

Scene 2

On stage: Magic bag. *In it*: reference book, spell book, wand
Off stage: 1 empty haversack (**Seth**)
1 full haversack containing warm clothing, Smarties in outer pocket (**Seth**)
Personal: **Seth**: dolly mixtures
Salmonella: magic telescope

Furniture and Property List 47

SCENE 3

On stage: Nil

Off stage: Jam pan (**Urgle**)
Large wooden spoon (**Urgle**)
Enormous strawberries (**Urgle**)
Chalice with lid (**Urgle**)
Chalice with lid (**Chief Urgle**)

SCENE 4

On stage: Cave entrance UL
Rocks and stones scattered on ground
Cave exit UR. *Near it*: large rock

Off stage: Travel bag containing picnic, warm clothing, rug (**Crystal**)
Rock, travel bag containing specimen jars, labels, jelly babies (**Professor**)
2 firestones (**Guardian**)
2 firestones (**Guardian**)
Magic bag containing spell book, telescope, wand, aerosol (**Salmonella**)
Full haversack (**Seth**)

SCENE 5

On stage: Vegetation DL

Off stage: Travel bag containing picnic, warm clothing, rug (**Crystal**)
Travel bag containing specimen jars, labels, jelly babies (**Professor**)
Magic bag (**Salmonella**)
Full haversack (**Seth**)

Personal: **Salmonella**: dolly mixtures
Professor: caterpillar

SCENE 6

On stage: Snow

Off stage: Deckchair, snowflake machine, travel brochures, radio, alarm clock (**Snowflake Maker**)
Magic bag, **Professor**'s bag, **Crystal**'s bag—all with contents as before (**Seth**)

Personal: **Crystal**: handkerchief
Professor: map and compass

ACT II

Scene 1

On stage: Ravaged strawberry plants
Footprint (optional) DL

Off stage: Full haversack, magic bag, **Professor**'s bag containing jelly babies (**Seth**)
Travel bag (**Crystal**)
Chalice of jam with lid (**Chief Urgle**)

Personal: **Professor**: magnifying glass, tape measure, notebook
Urgles: dagger each
Crystal: Whooperdink feather

Scene 2

On stage: Snow
Deckchair C with travel brochures
Snowflake machine DR

Personal: **Professor**: magnifying glass

Scene 3

On stage: Cage C. *On floor*: **Professor**'s bag containing bottle marked "sulphuric acid", **Crystal**'s bag, full haversack, magic bag containing spell book, feather lightly coated with fluorescent paint

Personal: **Seth**: magic snowflake
Urgle guards: spears

Scene 4

On stage: Cave entrance UR. *Near it*: large rock
Rocks and stones scattered on ground

Personal: **Professor**: chalice of jam with lid in pocket, magnifying glass

Scene 5

On stage: Snow
Deckchair C with travel brochures
Snowflake machine DR

Off stage: Full haversack, magic bag, **Crystal**'s bag, **Professor**'s bag containing Polaroid 2000 camera with rigged photo of **Professor** and **Whooperdink** and rigged photo of **Urgles** (**Seth**)
Magic snow (**Stage Management** or **Snowflake Maker**)

Personal: **Crystal**: magic snowflake
Professor: 3 magic snowflakes

LIGHTING PLOT

Property fittings required: nil
Various simple interior and exterior settings

ACT I SCENE 1

To open:	Full general lighting	
Cue 1	**Professor** and **Crystal** exit *Fade to Black-out*	(Page 4)

ACT I SCENE 2

To open:	Full general lighting	
Cue 2	**Salmonella**: ". . . spell I was making." *Fade to green spot on* **Salmonella**	(Page 6)
Cue 3	**Voice**: ". . . will make him bright." *Lighting up to full, fade green spot*	(Page 7)
Cue 4	**Seth** runs off after **Salmonella** *Fade to Black-out*	(Page 8)

ACT I SCENE 3

To open:	General blue lighting	
Cue 5	As all **Urgles** exit to end scene *Fade to Black-out*	(Page 9)

ACT I SCENE 4

To open:	Full general lighting	
Cue 6	**Guardian** enters *Red spot on* **Guardian**	(Page 10)
Cue 7	**Guardian** exits *Fade red spot, change lighting to give new landscape effect*	(Page 11)
Cue 8	**Professor** and **Crystal** exit DR *Full general lighting as at scene opening*	(Page 11)
Cue 9	**Guardian** enters *Red spot on* **Guardian**	(Page 13)
Cue 10	**Guardian** exits into cave UL *Fade red spot, change lighting to give new landscape effect*	(Page 15)

| Cue 11 | **Salmonella** and **Seth** exit DR
Fade to Black-out | (Page 15) |

ACT I SCENE 5

| *To open*: | Lighting for new landscape effect | |
| Cue 12 | End of "The Whooperdink" song
Fade to Black-out | (Page 19) |

ACT I SCENE 6

To open:	Snowflake effect	
Cue 13	As **Snowflake Maker** begins to speak *Lights slowly up to full*	(Page 19)
Cue 14	**Crystal**: " ... a song called 'Snowflake'." *Fade to snowflake effect*	(Page 22)
Cue 15	End of "Snowflake" song *Lighting up to full as before*	(Page 22)
Cue 16	**Professor, Crystal, Salmonella** and **Seth** exit *Fade to snowflake effect then Black-out*	(Page 23)

ACT II SCENE 1

| *To open*: | General blue lighting | |
| Cue 17 | **Crystal, Seth,** and the **Urgles** exit
Fade to Black-out | (Page 30) |

ACT II SCENE 2

To open:	Snowflake effect	
Cue 18	**Whooperdink** enters *Full general lighting*	(Page 30)
Cue 19	**Snowflake Maker**: "The green-faced old goat." *Pause, then fade to snowflake effect*	(Page 32)
Cue 20	**Snowflake Maker** drifts off into a reverie *Fade to Black-out*	(Page 33)

ACT II SCENE 3

To open:	Black-out	
Cue 21	**Crystal**: "Don't worry, Seth, I'm here." *Bring up general dim lighting with spot on* **Crystal** *and* **Seth** C	(Page 33)
Cue 22	**Seth** shrugs. Pause *Ultra-violet light on so that feather glows*	(Page 33)
Cue 23	**Voice**: " ... will make him bright." *Ultra-violet light off*	(Page 34)

Lighting Plot

Cue 24	**Seth** and **Crystal** pick up bags *Bring up lighting to give dawn effect*	(Page 36)
Cue 25	**Seth, Crystal, Chief Urgle** and **Urgles** exit *Fade to Black-out*	(Page 36)

ACT II SCENE 4

To open:	New landscape effect lighting	
Cue 26	**Guardian** enters *Red spot on* **Guardian**	(Page 36)
Cue 27	**Guardian** exits *Fade red spot*	(Page 37)
Cue 28	**Professor, Salmonella** and **Whooperdink** exit *Fade to Black-out*	(Page 39)

ACT II SCENE 5

To open:	Snowflake effect	
Cue 29	**Crystal**: "There he is." *Bring up lighting to full*	(Page 39)
Cue 30	All exit *Fade to Black-out*	(Page 45)

EFFECTS PLOT

ACT I

Cue 1	**Professor**'s experiment explodes *Loud bang and explosion effect from bench*	(Page 1)
Cue 2	**Salmonella**: "... spell I was making." *Eerie forest sounds*	(Page 6)
Cue 3	**Salmonella**: "... all was still." *Eerie forest sounds stop*	(Page 6)
Cue 4	**Salmonella**: "... from the skies." *Echoed* **Voice** *recites the curse as in text*	(Page 6)
Cue 5	**Salmonella** points at **Seth** *Flash*	(Page 7)
Cue 6	**Salmonella** points at **Seth** *Flash*	(Page 8)
Cue 7	**Chief Urgle** exists with chalice *Pause, then slurping noise*	(Page 9)
Cue 8	**Professor** throws stone into cave UL *Red flash from inside cave* UL	(Page 11)
Cue 9	**Crystal** throws stone into cave UL *Red flash from inside cave* UL	(Page 11)
Cue 10	**Seth** throws stone into cave UL *Red flash from inside cave* UL	(Page 14)
Cue 11	**Seth** drops false stone inside cave UL *Red flash from inside cave* UL	(Page 15)
Cue 12	**Salmonella** throws real stone into cave UR *Green flash from inside cave* UR	(Page 15)
Cue 13	**Snowflake Maker**: "Thank you." *Alarm clock rings, cut as* **Snowflake Maker** *stops alarm*	(Page 23)
Cue 14	As **Snowflake Maker** switches on radio *Desert-island type music*	(Page 23)
Cue 15	**Salmonella** points wand at radio *Tune distorted by crackling and hissing*	(Page 23)

Effects Plot

ACT II

Cue 16	**Seth** wipes away tears *Eerie forest sounds, echoed* **Voice** *as in text, then stop eerie forest sounds*	(Page 34)
Cue 17	**Snowflake Maker** throws magic snowflake *Shower of magic snow over* **Salmonella** *and magic sound*	(Page 41)
Cue 18	**Snowflake Maker** throws magic snowflake *Shower of magic snow and magic sound*	(Page 42)
Cue 19	**Snowflake Maker** throws magic snowflake *Shower of magic snow and magic sound*	(Page 44)
Cue 20	**Snowflake Maker** throws magic snowflake *Shower of magic snow and magic sound*	(Page 44)

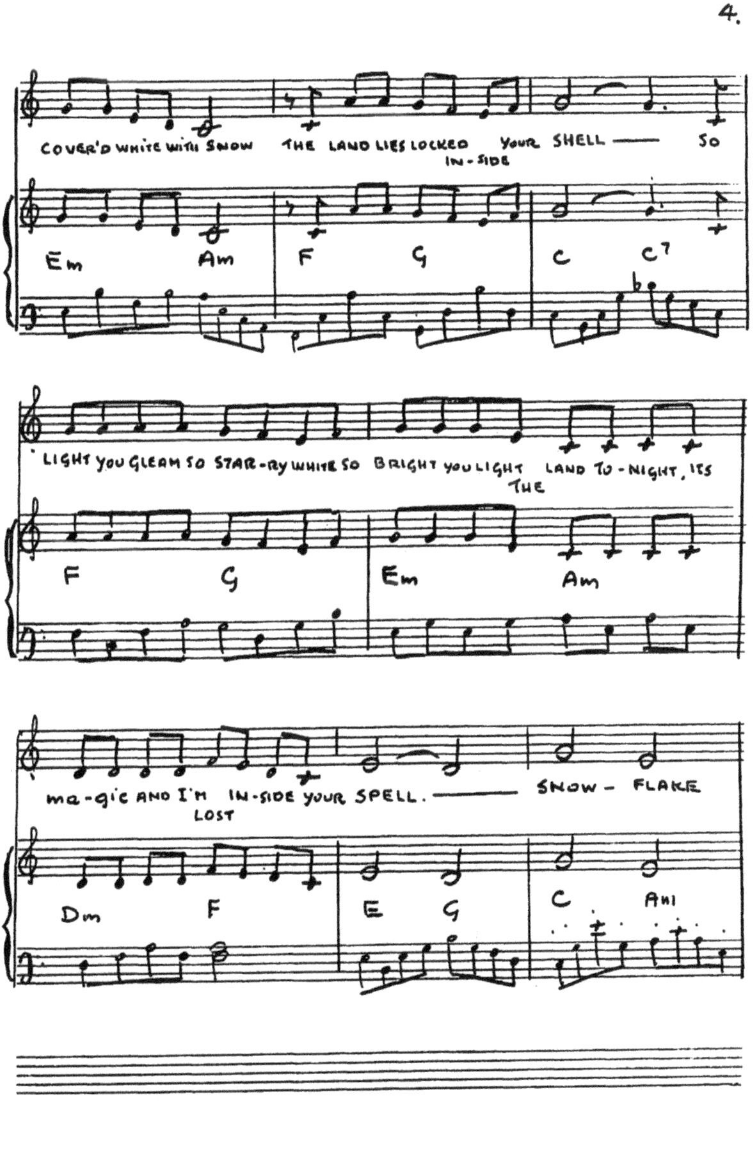
4.
COVER'D WHITE WITH SNOW THE LAND LIES LOCKED YOUR SHELL —— SO
IN-SIDE
Em Am F G C C7
LIGHT YOU GLEAM SO STAR-RY WHITE SO BRIGHT YOU LIGHT LAND TO-NIGHT, ITS
THE
F G Em Am
ma-gic AND I'M IN-SIDE YOUR SPELL. ——— SNOW - FLAKE
LOST
Dm F E G C Am

6.

www.ingramcontent.com/pod-product-compliance
Ingram Content Group UK Ltd.
Pitfield, Milton Keynes, MK11 3LW, UK
UKHW021847210426
5322IPUK00022B/514